# reach within

## educational manual

a guide to building self-esteem
through connection and movement

 iUniverse

# REACH WITHIN EDUCATIONAL MANUAL
## A GUIDE TO BUILDING SELF-ESTEEM THROUGH CONNECTION AND MOVEMENT

*iUniverse books may be ordered through booksellers or by contacting:*

*iUniverse*
*1663 Liberty Drive*
*Bloomington, IN 47403*
*www.iuniverse.com*
*1-800-Authors (1-800-288-4677)*

*Because of the dynamic nature of the Internet, any web addresses or links contained in this book may have changed since publication and may no longer be valid. The views expressed in this work are solely those of the author and do not necessarily reflect the views of the publisher, and the publisher hereby disclaims any responsibility for them.*

*Any people depicted in stock imagery provided by Thinkstock are models, and such images are being used for illustrative purposes only. Certain stock imagery © Thinkstock.*

*ISBN: 978-1-4917-8309-2 (sc)*
*ISBN: 978-1-4917-8310-8 (e)*

*Library of Congress Control Number: 2015919834*

*Print information available on the last page.*

*iUniverse rev. date: 04/05/2016*

**reachwithin** is a multi-faceted program that aims to improve the lives of children impacted by prior early life adversity. **reachwithin** is a psychosocial, educational and mindfulness-based program for children and their caregivers which may be delivered in individual or group settings. This program encourages healthy interpersonal development and relationships by promoting self-regulation, emotional literacy and social skills, all of which contribute to lasting resilience. The **reachwithin** philosophy originates from the belief that children's healthy development is dependent on meaningful and consistent attachments to adults and other children. We believe that a child's personal fulfillment in school, play and all activities depends on a sense of belonging under conditions of safety, security and comfort.

**reachwithin's** mission is to improve the health and wellbeing of vulnerable, at-risk children, especially those living in residential care facilities or non-biologic homes. A fundamental objective of the program is to help at-risk children be better able to regulate their emotions and their relationships through thought and action by engaging in mindful interactions.

Additionally, our methodology focuses on educating caregivers to help at-risk children develop and grow into secure, healthy adults. Above all, we hope to plant seeds for their happiness within a context of self-worth, competence, and calm nurturing. Our training informs caregivers on ways to approach this monumental task by providing them with trauma-informed and child development-informed approaches and activities that will help them create healthier interactions while caring for this special population, including when to use appropriate positive disciplinary methods. Our hope is that however slowly or quickly change happens, children and their caregivers work together as a team with a shared sense of purpose and trust. If joy is the ultimate end goal, the steps along the way should be fun, interactive and socially rewarding. Though there are certain to be moments of painful retreat into habitual behaviors of self-protection, we know too, that the simple reminder "if there is no challenge, there can be no change" will keep both child and caregiver on track.

This manual includes an informational workbook for caregivers and is accompanied by lesson plans to adapt for use with children in various settings. The lessons may facilitate discussions about children's experiences and enable them to describe, understand and over time regulate their emotions. These lessons also aim to improve social awareness, interactions and relationships between both caregiver and children so that they may become better able to empathize with others they come in contact with outside of this therapeutic milieu.

We hope that children and caregivers participating in the **reachwithin** program will enjoy gaining these important life skills towards reclaiming their birthrights of fulfilled potentials.

Karen Lawson, Ph.D.
Co-Founder and Director
**reachwithin**

# Table of Contents

I. About **reachwithin**    6
Who we are? • What is **reachwithin**? • Dedication and Acknowledgements • Disclaimer

II. Overview    8
About this manual • Population overview

III. The **reachwithin** Model    12
Objectives • Theory • Format

IV. Information for Facilitators: The Basics    18
What does it mean to be a facilitator? • Mental health basics • Yoga basics • Group basics

V. Information for Facilitators: Communication skills    24
Compassionate communication • Active listening • Nonviolent communication
Communicating with children • Cultural compatibility and language

VI. Information for Facilitators: Boundaries and Consistency    29
Healthy boundaries • Consistency • Transitions and losses

VII. Information for Facilitators: Behavior management    34
Behavior management • Tips from Facilitators • What to expect in child development

VIII. Self-care and stress    41

IX. Program Assessment    44

X. Resources    45

XI. Appendices/Supplements    46
- Appendix A: Theory sources
- Appendix B: Child development chart
- Appendix C: Facilitator Tips, dos and don'ts
- Appendix D: Accommodating special situations: Pregnancy, Injury and Obesity
- Appendix E: Yoga poses
- Appendix F: Yoga postures and breathing for specific situations
- Appendix G: **reachwithin** Assessment Tool

XII. References    73

XIII. Glossary    74

XIV. Lessons (see also lesson document for complete lesson plans)    75
Preparation for class • Sample lessons organized by theme area

# I. About reachwithin

The Bartholomew J. Lawson Foundation for Children, a US based 501(c)(3), created REACH Grenada in 2008 as a principle program to specifically improve the health and wellbeing of Grenada's most vulnerable youth. **reachwithin** is a multi-faceted program developed to improve the lives of formerly maltreated children living in residential care facilities in Grenada. The program teaches valuable skills to support children in leading empowered lives and overcoming adversity. **reachwithin** is a 12 session, group experience for children that builds resilience and promotes positive relationships through the development of self-regulation, emotional literacy and social skills. In 2013 the name REACH Grenada was changed to **reachwithin** due to program interest from other Caribbean islands.

## Acknowledgements

### reachwithin Manual Contributors

Primary:
Lindsay Haffner Eagleton RYT 200, RCYT
Moira Hennessey Ph.D., MPH
Stephanie Holmes RYT 200
Richard Honigman M.D., FAAP
Karen Lawson Ph.D.
Erin Wilson RYT
Aliza Yarrow Psy.D.

Secondary:
Vincent Aloi
Anna Chobor
Kathy Jackson
Barbara Landon Psy.D.
Sharon Lickerman M.Ed.
Katie Moran
Neo Satyam Moreton, RYT
Charlotte Munson
Lauren Orlando
Marije E. Paternotte RYT
Katie Randall RYT 200

Design and Art Direction by Azita Panahpour
Yoga Illustrations by Michele Rosenthal
Layout Design by
Kimball Richmond and Elena Zaharakos

Special thanks to the following people for their support and guidance given to **reachwithin** through the years: T. Berry Brazelton M.D., Joshua D. Sparrow M.D., Maria Trozzi M.S., Hazel DaBreo Ph.D., and especially Mrs. Marion Pierre

## Dedication

This manual is dedicated to the inspiring children, staff and directors of Grenada's children's homes who have participated in our youth program and inspired its growth and evolution. Thank you for allowing us to participate in your lives.

We would like to thank Bart, Mackenzie and Katia Lawson for their shining example of resilience and for their participation in building **reachwithin**.

## Disclaimer

The exercises and information in this manual are meant to be tools but not treatment or assessments for mental or emotional conditions. If you suspect that a participant in your group is experiencing a clinical condition such as Post-Traumatic Stress Disorder, please consult with a doctor, mental health specialist or child protection professional.

Not all exercises are suitable for everyone. Please adjust to your level and the level of your class. To reduce the risk of injury, never force or strain; always listen to your body and watch your participants. If you or people in your class experience pain or discomfort during this exercise, stop immediately and consult a doctor. The instruction presented is a guide and a suggestion. It is neither a prescription nor a substitute for medical advice.

# II. Overview

## About this manual

This manual is a workbook guide for youth program facilitators and caregivers taking part in a **reachwithin** training program. In this manual you will find information about working with at-risk youth, a review of yoga basics, a rationale for the program's model, as well as teaching instructions, lesson plans and resources for leading a **reachwithin** youth program at your site or in your community. This manual should be used in conjunction with attending a **reachwithin** training workshop where the material is explored in greater detail and skills for facilitators are practiced and discussed.

Use the manual, experience and knowledge you gain from a **reachwithin** training workshop as a framework to create your own program that you can adjust to meet the specific needs of your setting, population, and resources.

> *Ask yourself:*
> * What do I hope to get out of reading this manual?
> * What will be helpful about this program for the children I work with?

## Population Overview: Vulnerable and At-Risk Youth

**reachwithin** was created to help youth in residential care facilities develop skills and draw on internal resources to build strength and overall wellbeing. You may find it helpful to use this manual with a wide range of vulnerable or at-risk youth, including survivors of trauma. **reachwithin** can be delivered in care facilities, community centers, and schools.

### Who are at-risk youth?

"At-risk" youth, also called "vulnerable" youth, is a broad category. The term includes children who are living in difficult circumstances that threaten healthy growth and development. Vulnerable youth include: children separated from their caregivers (due to illness, death, incarceration or maltreatment), children experiencing abuse or neglect, children who have experienced other trauma (including domestic or community violence, war or natural disasters), children who become homeless or "street" children, and children growing up in poverty or witnessing violence.

Children can be extremely resilient. Being resilient means having the ability to appropriately manage or recover from difficulties and/or challenges in life. With more and more negative experiences, however, one's adaptive resources can become overwhelmed. This is more likely to lead to unhealthy outcomes or chronic problems. Working with new at-risk youth or those who have not had a chance to receive adequate intervention(s), you may see some or all of the following negative outcomes becoming established: low self-esteem, relationship and attachment difficulties, drug use, age-inappropriate sexual behaviors, aggression, mental health difficulties and/or behavioral issues .

You can promote health and decrease the likelihood of negative outcomes by promoting adaptive management (coping) techniques and supporting children in using their natural strengths and internal resources.

> **Ask yourself:**
> - What does it mean for children in my community to be vulnerable?
> - In my job or community, what experiences lead to children being at-risk?
> - What sort of strengths and natural coping resources did I draw on as a child?
> - What coping skills do I see the children I work with using? Are they adaptive or maladaptive?

## Understanding Types of Vulnerable Youth

### Children living outside the home:

In the best of circumstances "home" (however that is defined in the child's culture, including living with biologic parents) provides children with a sense of safety, caring support, and attention that allows them to grow, know themselves and engage in healthy relationship development. Living outside of the "home" often involves frequent changes of residence, disruptions in safety, security, learning, as well as less attention and less consistent long term healthy relationships. This is especially the case for youth in child welfare systems who have been removed from their homes due to abuse or neglect.

You may see problems in physical growth and/or emotional development among children in the aforementioned circumstances. In the child welfare system, five times as many children are observed to have developmental, emotional or behavioral problems as compared to other children in the community (Caulsen et al., 1998; Landsverk et al., 2009). For example, an assessment in the Caribbean found that over 60% of children living in group foster homes showed significant emotional or behavioral difficulties, and over 80% had experienced trauma (REACH Grenada, 2011). So what is it about being away from home that causes so much developmental disruption for children?

Once removed from their homes, children in child welfare systems often experience stress from being away from the family they have known even if they lived in adverse circumstances. They often experience multiple, drastic changes, such as housing changes, school disruptions or changes, separation from friends, and loss of familiar environment as well as changes in schedules and activities. Also, they receive less one-to-one attention than children living in stable family settings. There is a loss of reliable, predictable, respectful patterned interactions that enable a healthy developing child to feel supported, safe and secure. That is partly why children living in residential group homes appear to have poorer mental wellbeing, social and/or behavioral functioning than children in kinship care or foster placements in communities (Cooper, J.L., Banghart, P., Aratani, P., 2010).

The longer children remain in the child welfare system, the more likely they are to experience problems in growth and healthy development. However, it is likely that a large portion of the mental health problems that these children develop have to do with the past trauma, maltreatment or neglect which originally led them to be identified by child protective agencies.

*Ask Yourself:*
- What does home mean to me?
- What is a traditional "home environment" like for children in the community I serve?
- For children not living at "home," where do they go?
- What kinds of experiences lead to difficulties for children in my community or work setting who no longer live at "home?"
- What is something I can do to help children experience a sense of home away from home?

## Children experiencing trauma:

Unfortunately trauma in childhood is not uncommon. Research tells us that 14 to 43 percent of children have experienced at least one traumatic event. Childhood trauma can result from anything that makes a child feel helpless and disrupts their sense of safety and security. This may include: sexual, physical or verbal abuse, domestic violence, an unstable or unsafe environment, separation from a parent, bullying, and serious illness or injury.

Not all children exposed to a traumatic event will have negative outcomes. Many different factors contribute to whether or not a child develops negative outcomes from a traumatic experience—also called traumatic stress. A child's age and developmental level, life history, strengths and weaknesses, or access to a supportive caregiver are some of the factors that pertain to children's responses to trauma and later outcomes. Children living in adversity, like poverty or violence, are at higher risk for negative outcomes due to trauma.

Traumatic stress can be disruptive to a child's growth in many ways, but is different for every child. Trauma can have a direct impact on the structural and functional development of children's brains and bodies. Traumatic stress can make it hard for children to concentrate, learn, and perform in school. It can also make it difficult for them to make and maintain healthy relationships. Trauma often changes how children view the world, their futures, and may lead to chronic health and/or behavioral problems over time.

*Ask yourself:*
- What types of trauma do children I work with commonly experience?
- How do I see the children I work with actively coping with their experiences?
- What are some of the coping behaviors I remember seeing children use?
- Are there any behaviors that I find difficult in the children I work with? How might these behaviors be related to traumatic stress?
- What are some ways that I have learned to cope with some of the difficult things I've experienced in my own life?

**Children in poverty:**
Growing up in extreme poverty is a big source of stress and vulnerability for youth. Psychological research has shown that living in poverty can have negative effects on the physical and mental health and well-being of children around the world.

Overall, children who grow up in poverty are exposed to more trauma, and often have less access to education and healthcare. Children in poverty are at risk for poorer academic performance, more health problems, and worse malnutrition. They are also at greater risk of behavioral and emotional problems (including anxiety, depression, hyperactivity and aggression). Children who live in poverty sometimes also live in unsafe neighborhoods that expose them to violence; this puts children at greater risk of injury, entry into juvenile justice system, and mortality.

Living in poverty is also particularly difficult for parents. Living in poverty in adulthood may result in overwhelming stress on a day-to-day basis. Parents dealing with poverty and stress often use harsh parenting and discipline techniques. Harsh parenting styles are linked to poor social and emotional outcomes in children.

*Ask Yourself:*
- How do I see poverty playing a role with children in my community?
- Are there specific characteristics of children impacted by poverty in my community?
- Have the children I am working with experienced poverty from a young age? How do I think this history plays a role in their lives today?

# III. The reachwithin Model

Overall, **reachwithin** aims to: 1) promote well-being, 2) increase resiliency, and 3) decrease distress among vulnerable youth. We do this by providing children with an opportunity to build a sense of meaning and belief in themselves and their abilities. This is also referred to as self-efficacy. Our lessons offer activities where children get to be part of a group, build relationships, have fun and interact in a safe environment. Our instructions and activities are written to be sensitive to some of the difficult life experiences affected children may have had. They also focus on the current moment and building skills.

## Objectives:

Many of the lessons target specific objectives or goals. These include:
1. Increasing emotional literacy
2. Improving self-regulation
3. Enhancing social skills

Emotional literacy refers to the ability to identify and understand feelings and emotions. Self-regulation refers to the ability to notice and tolerate difficult feelings, and manage mood or behavior. Social skills refer to the ability to communicate with others, form relationships, and participate in community in a pro-social adaptive manner.

> ### Ask Yourself:
> - Naming and understanding emotions can be complicated and difficult. Is knowing what I'm feeling easy or difficult for me in my own life? Do I notice this being easy or difficult for the children I work with?
> - Name three things I do for myself when I'm experiencing a difficult emotion. (These are the ways I engage in self-regulation.) How do these help me?
> - Think of three ways I am a great communicator. What are the social skills I use every day? How do these help me?

## Theory-base:

The ideas and work of many talented people working successfully with children around the world helped to shape the **reachwithin** model. Several different viewpoints and specific exercises were incorporated in developing our multi-dimensional approach towards working with youth. For more information on these sources, please see Appendix A.

When working with children, especially at-risk children, one usually comes in with their own ideas or theories about what helps children and how to understand their behavior. Use your own experience and understanding alongside the ideas you will find in this manual. Please be mindful that trauma survivors live with a deep sense of mistrust; being friendly and supportive is obviously necessary but will not by itself solve their issues.

## Framework:

Each of the twelve lesson topics are designed to help children gain skills in certain areas. Examples of these areas include: self-acceptance, healthy boundaries, and anger management.

With the children in your community, you might decide to use an entire lesson, or certain sections of a lesson, as seems appropriate for your group setting or time constraints. If you are using the program as a whole, the lessons are written with the purpose of being taught in order. This is because the lesson topics build on each other and what was taught in the previous session. In each session, do highlight the importance of community, safety, self-awareness, regulation and relationships.

The twelve lesson topics include:

### Lesson Plan Outline by Topic Areas
Topic 1- Healthy Boundaries- "We set boundaries to feel safe"
Topic 2- Mindfulness/Present Moment- "We notice what's going on inside and around us"
Topic 3 - Choices- "We are making choices all the time"
Topic 4 - Self-Regulation- "We can learn to control our actions"
Topic 5 – Caring and Empathy- "We can listen and share"
Topic 6 - Self-Acceptance-"We all have strengths"
Topic 7 – Emotional Awareness- "We all have feelings"
Topic 8 – Positive Thinking- "We can think in helpful ways"
Topic 9 - Anger Management- "We can control our anger and communicate what we want"
Topic 10 – Conflict Resolution- "We work together to solve problems"
Topic 11 – Coping/Moving Forward- "We can care for ourselves when hard things happen"
Topic 12 – Goals – "We have hopes and dreams"

## Format:

The **reachwithin** lesson manual has 12 topic areas. Each topic area includes two to four primary lesson activities. The **reachwithin** model was designed to be delivered weekly using a different lesson activity each week but can be adjusted to a shorter or longer time frame based on the needs of your site. Additional activities can be added or for shorter programs, you can delete one or two of the activities for each lesson area. The program can always be repeated to create opportunities for children to gain greater appreciation and exploration of the topics covered. If you decide to shorten the program, be sure to create opportunities for children to apply the material outside of the group sessions and have time to understand the topic material. On the other hand, if you lead the program over a longer period of time, be sure to review the concepts and topics that have already be covered when introducing new lesson topics.

Whenever possible, it is best for children to attend all of the group sessions from start to finish, so that they can form relationships and build trust in the group. However, this may not be possible for your setting. If consistent participation and attendance is not possible, review group rules at the beginning of each session, conduct weekly introductions of yourself and other group members, and focus on building relationships whenever possible. These reminders are helpful for all children, but they are particularly important for children that have experienced trauma. This is because consistency and knowing what to expect allows children to stay better regulated and engaged in the group activities.

In terms of facilitators in the group, it is best to have at least two adults involved in each group, so the group will not be disrupted if one adult needs to leave the room or help an individual child. You may want to have the two adults act as co-facilitators (taking turns leading the activities or groups), or have one adult act as the head facilitator (leading the groups) and the other adult playing a supporting role. Choose whatever is possible and most likely to be successful at your site. Successful group facilitators show an ability to connect well with children, have a sense of inner calm and peace, demonstrate respect for children's emotions, and are familiar with yoga postures and games. Facilitator's attendance at each session is important to address attachment and trauma-related dynamics necessary for children to learn and grow.

*Ask yourself:*
- Who might be available to be a consistent group facilitator in my setting?
- What qualities do these group facilitators have that would lead to a successful group experience?
- What might be challenging for these group facilitators in leading such a group?
- Will I choose to have two co-facilitators, or one leading and one supporting facilitator? Why will this be the best choice for the site or children I am working with?

In terms of group size, we recommend having about 10 children in each group. Fifteen children in a group should be the absolute maximum. When deciding how many children to have in your groups, think about the needs of your setting. Make sure to think about the behavior and ability of the children you work with. Smaller groups are recommended for children with more behavioral difficulties. Larger groups may be possible when more facilitators are available, or children have experienced working and playing successfully in structured groups. In general, but especially for large groups, it will be helpful to make smaller groups during different lessons or lesson activities to address topics in greater depth. This would allow the children to relate to different children in the different groups, therefore improving social interactions.

Organize your groups by age and developmental level of the children you are working with. The following age breakdowns may be helpful guidelines for the groups of children you may be working with: toddler to 5 years of age; 6 to 11 years; and adolescents 12+ years. You may notice that children of the same age might have very different abilities based on their individual development and life experiences. Pay attention to the strengths, capabilities and challenges of children in your setting when deciding who should be in each group. Younger children are often comfortable in mixed gender groups (meaning boys and girls together), but adolescents (or teens) often prefer to meet in single-gender groups.

In terms of the length of time for groups, we outline a 60 minute session. However, for older children the length of time can be extended to 90 minutes or shortened to 45 minutes for younger children. You may adjust the length of sessions depending on how often you run your groups. If you're running the group less often (for example: every-other-week), longer sessions are recommended. Shorter sessions are recommended if you are running groups more often (example: more than once-a-week). We recommend that you plan sessions for weekends or after school hours when children will be best able to focus on the activities.

Children will learn the most from the lessons if we help them to apply the material they are learning about in between group meetings. Feel free to create these opportunities for the children in your groups, or suggest a "homework" task for each lesson. If you decide to create follow-up or homework activities, be sure to follow up by letting staff know about what the children will be doing to practice what they learned outside of the group.

## Group Session Structure

**reachwithin** group sessions should follow a similar structured framework for every session in order for children to anticipate what will be happening from week-to-week.

Each group lesson starts with an opening time, so that children can know what they will be working on during the group session. Next, yoga postures and a yoga game as the physical activity series will help children release energy and focus. Then the group activity for the session will focus on skill building related to the topic area of the lesson. After the activity, a relaxation or meditation time follows so children can calm themselves and reflect on the topic. Finally, the group facilitators lead a closing of the day's group, where they summarize and reinforce the lesson topic and messages. This is also a time when facilitators and children can talk about how to practice the skills they learned outside of the group (as "homework"). In the lessons included, these activities vary from topic to topic, however, having some of the pieces of each lesson be consistent for children may be helpful. For each lesson topic area, think about maintaining one type of warm-up, physical activity or meditation, for the several group lessons you may have for a given topic area in order to help children become comfortable and gain mastery over those specific activities before moving on to others. Repetition can help benefit by deepening the group experience, as children and adults (especially those who have experienced trauma) thrive best in safe, patterned and predictable environments.

> *Ask yourself:*
> * What routines might be helpful in my group sessions?
> * Are there any healthy procedures that children already engage in that can be drawn upon during my group sessions?
> * What has been the role of routine and pattern in my life?

## Lesson Plan Format

| ACTIVITIES | DIRECTIONS | TIME/RESOURCES |
|---|---|---|
| OPENING | Check in and introduce topic by facilitator | 5 minutes (lesson plan, teaching points) |
| YOGA | Yoga postures and yoga game | 15 minutes (yoga postures, mats, etc.) |
| ACTIVITY | Group, individual or partner activity that focuses on skill building by theme | 25 minutes (worksheet, activity materials, mental health activity) |
| RELAXATION/MEDITATION | Relaxation, meditation or journaling | 10 minutes (music and mat, personal space, etc.) |
| CLOSING | Sharing and review (Possible hw) | 10 minutes (participation and teaching points) |
| (add "homework" between sessions if it's right for your site) | (varied) | (varied, about 10-15 minutes outside of group time) |

Time for each piece of the lesson plan will vary slightly based on specific tasks and decisions you make about the length of the group sessions.

# IV. Information for Facilitators: The Basics

*Ask Yourself:*
- Thinking back to important or good teachers in my life, what qualities did they have? What helped me learn and engage in different classes?

## What does it mean to be a reachwithin facilitator?

By facilitating or leading a **reachwithin** program, you are assisting children and young people to learn about themselves, and to learn and practice skills to help them develop. As a facilitator you will be teaching new skills. However, you will also be learning alongside the children in your group. Everyone at a given **reachwithin** session is an active participant and can both learn and potentially share with others (or teach).

*Ask Yourself:*
- As an example for children, what qualities would I like to model for the children to learn?
- Who are the important models or examples in my life? What did I learn from them?

In your role as a facilitator with children, you act as a model or example. Do your best to model the activities, communication and attitude you would like to see among the children in your group. They will follow your lead in how to act in the group sessions. Ideally, you can act as a positive, respectful and non-judgmental example for the participants in the group. Many trauma survivors are highly attuned, sensitive and reactive to changes in the emotional states of others. Please take the time to make sure that you are in a calm and self-aware state before leading each session.

Working with at-risk youth uses a combination of skills, personality and knowledge, including patience and enthusiasm for what you are teaching, as well as an understanding of what the children you are working with are facing in their daily lives.

Past **reachwithin** facilitators had the following advice for working with at-risk youth:
- Create a safe group environment and lead the lessons with confidence
- Keep it real, mean what you say, be honest
- Provide encouragement and enthusiasm
- Observe and shift to the needs of children
- Give individual attention to children when possible
- Understand your personal boundaries
- Pay attention and listen to the children in your groups
- Be compassionate and show respect
- Be a model in what you say and do, including yoga postures and group exercises, and do the activities alongside the children and teens

- Be sure to praise the whole class for their efforts
- Enjoy yourself, be positive and have fun. If you are having fun, students will have fun!
- Create a routine that can be counted on
- Be curious about the experiences of kids in the group by asking questions
- Trust that doing your best will lead to a positive experience for the group!

*Ask Yourself:*
- Imagine leading a group or being a child in my own group. What other guidelines would I add to this list?

## Psychosocial Basics: What is well-being? What are coping skills?

*Ask yourself:*
- What routines might be helpful in my group sessions?
- Are there any healthy procedures that children already engage in that can be drawn upon during my group sessions?
- What has been the role of routine and pattern in my life?

The World Health Organization describes health as "a state of complete physical, mental and social well-being and not merely the absence of disease or infirmity" (World Health Organization, 2011). Mental health, specifically, is often defined as a state of well-being that allows people to realize their potential, cope with normal stresses of everyday life, work or learn productively, and contribute to their communities (World Health Organization, 2014). Health and well-being are especially important for children since they are constantly learning and developing their world view and their place in it.

We can help improve the overall health of children by supporting their social and emotional well-being, as this is the foundation for healthy development.

*Ask yourself:*
- When I think back to my experience as a child, I notice that I coped with challenges and difficulties by: _____
- How have I noticed other people or children coping with stress and problems?

One way to support children's emotional and social well-being is through encouraging children to learn and use adaptive coping skills. Coping skills refer to skills, techniques and behaviors/actions we use to help us adjust to change and manage stressors or demands of everyday life. By using a variety of adaptive coping skills, children can increase their resilience. Resilience refers to a child's ability to "bounce back" from stress and difficult life experiences. Other important lessons for trauma survivors to learn are that they have a choice and that they have control over their bodies.

Building resilience is especially important for "at-risk" youth because they experience a great deal of ongoing stress and/or have had overwhelming (or traumatic) experiences.

## Yoga Basics: What is Yoga? What is not Yoga? How does it help children?

### YOGA BASICS

Physical exercise is important for children and their healthy development. Children can be physically active in many different ways. One way is called yoga. People have different ideas about what yoga is. It is believed that yoga first originated in India nearly 5000 years ago. For **reachwithin**, yoga means physical postures and breathing exercises that are good for both the body and the mind.

In yoga, we teach children breathing techniques that build skills that help with self-regulation and self-control. For the yoga exercises taught in **reachwithin**, the idea is that the yoga skills learned in the group sessions can easily be taken "off the yoga mat" and into the everyday lives of children to help them deal with adversity or challenges that may encounter. Also, practicing yoga can help with strength, flexibility, and overall well-being.

Yoga is appropriate for children of all ages. In the lesson plans, you will find yoga postures and yoga games. Yoga games are a fun way for kids to experience and learn yoga. This is especially important when teaching kids, as they learn best when they are having fun! We have created four unique yoga sequences that are included in the lesson plans

## Helpful Hints for beginning a yoga practice.

Yoga is a special form of exercise, because in addition to physical activity, it helps children practice breathing, mindfulness, self-acceptance, self-regulation and be comfortable with their bodies. This helps children learn how to calm and soothe their bodies and minds when stressed or upset. Here are a few helpful hints to keep in mind when practicing or leading yoga.

**Be gentle with your body**. Work to find a balance between working hard and feeling comfortable in each position or exercise. You want to challenge your body, but not strain it. If you feel a pain or strain in a posture, gently ease off. Postures should be fun and flexible—there is no need to compete with yourself or others.

**Focus on Your Breath**. Focus on breathing in each movement and position. This helps calm your mind and build focus and concentration while calming and strengthening your body. If you notice your mind wandering, focus on your breathing and the way your body feels.

Even though survivors of trauma may have difficulty with breathing calmly at rest, the pairing of breath control with physical activity can be more comforting.

**Practice Yoga Skills Often.** The best way to understand yoga and build the necessary skills is to practice often. The more you practice yoga, the better your teaching will become. The best way to teach is to teach by example. Children will learn a lot about yoga through your example of doing the postures and games together.

### Why might Yoga be helpful for children?

The children you work with experience many stressors. Yoga is helpful for reducing stress, and provides an opportunity to release physical energy. It is also helpful to calm the mind and help with feelings. Yoga provides practical tools for youth to self-regulate and is a means for them to gain control over their health and wellbeing. Children can use these tools for the rest of their lives. For instance, yoga instructors have observed and shared that yoga can help kids by:
- Increasing strength, flexibility, and improving coordination and balance
- Increasing body awareness and helping to build a healthy body image
- Reducing stress, anxiety and depression
- Improving quality of sleep
- Creating a healthy outlet for excess energy and nervousness

*Ask yourself:*
- In what ways do I imagine yoga will be helpful for the children I work with?
- Do I think the children I work with would enjoy an exercise-based activity? What aspects of physical movement might they like or benefit from?
- In what ways do I imagine physical exercises or movement may be a challenge for the children at my site?

## Group Basics: Why use a group format for children and adolescents?

For children and adolescents (and even adults!), groups can provide a powerful, meaningful experience. Almost all of children's learning happens in groups, such as in school, sports, arts, and religious experiences. Because of this, children and adolescents are great at connecting with each other and learning in a group format. Groups can be a place for children to find support from each other and the group facilitator. In a group that feels safe, children may feel comfortable sharing experiences and expressing feelings that they may not have felt able to share before. Groups offer a place to feel seen, heard, and understood by other children who may have had similar life experiences. Children can benefit from skill building groups. Some of these benefits might include feeling stronger, feeling less lonely, feeling better about themselves, and feeling more "normal", improving social skills and creative adaptive social bonds. Groups can be a powerful way for children to learn they're not alone—that there are others who are "like me."

Groups are most likely to feel safe to children when they accept kids for who they are, make the children feel welcome, are understanding of differences, and have clear rules and expectations.

> **Ask yourself:**
> - If I think back to my favorite group experience as a child, what made it so special?
> - In what ways was that experience different—maybe even better—because it was in a group?

**reachwithin** focuses on building skills and is a group, but it is not group therapy. One important difference is that in the group sessions you facilitate, the focus will not be on children sharing about their personal difficult or traumatic experiences. Instead they will focus on knowing themselves better, learning skills and connecting with others in a pro-social fashion.

Groups are an excellent way to help children with feelings and relationships. Groups can be especially helpful for children who have experienced teasing, bullying, or other forms of aggression. As children grow into adolescents, they usually turn to other teenagers for support—groups can give children a way to gain support from other teenagers, in the presence of caring adults who can help. (http://www.connectionscagp.com/)

> **Ask yourself:**
> - Think about the group experiences for children at my setting. In what ways have I seen these groups be a positive experience for the children I work with?
> - In what ways have groups been a challenging experience for the children I work with?

## Tips for a Successful Group Session

Sometimes groups can run so smoothly that it seems to happen without effort. Other groups need more guidance and help along the way. Either way, you might find the following tips useful when preparing for your group.

- Be prepared: be familiar with the activities and plans for the day, and have a sense of the lesson you want the group to learn.
- Actively engage: in successful groups the children might do more talking than the facilitators. Take time to introduce topics, but keep your introductions short and to-the-point to leave time for participants to discuss.
- Provide consistency: create a group structure/pattern so that children know what to expect from group-to-group. Routines and rituals can be very helpful.
- Share the plan: let the group know what to expect for the day.
- Be creative: if something isn't working, change it up!
- Notice energy: is the group tired, hyperactive, difficult to engage with or difficult to control? Check in with the energy level of the group, and change your plan depending on the group's energy. For a tired group, engage them in an activity that requires and builds energy. For a very energetic group that feels a little out-of-control, engage them in an energy-lowering activity—slowing down the group so they can really participate.

- Be flexible: while structure is important, if something is going really well or not-well, check in with the group about changing the structure to allow for more or less time with the activity. If the group agrees, and you've talked about the change, feel free to change-it-up!
- Set clear boundaries: the group should start and end on time, group rules and guidelines should be followed, and the role of the facilitator should be clear and expectable.
- Address problems: although groups can provide a wonderful space for connection, at some point some group members will have difficult moments with each other. It is important to address these as they happen with the individual group members involved, as well as the group as a whole. Open communication is important so that all group members can feel seen, heard, understood and respected.
- Have fun: make this a group goal—everyone gets more out of the group experience if group is enjoyable! Check in with yourself and with the group frequently—if it's no longer fun, ask the group about the what, when, why, and how of what's gone wrong, and work together to change things so that you're having fun again.

> **Ask yourself:**
> - What else do I want to add to this list to help run a successful group with the children I work with in my setting?

## Group Rules and Expectations

For each group you facilitate, make sure to focus on creating a safe space and promoting healthy boundaries. One important way to do this is to set the rules/expectations for the class in the first session. Creating and enforcing rules is extremely important in order to create a safe space with clear boundaries.

You may choose to create your own rules and share them with the group (recommended for groups of younger children) or create rules/ expectations with the children's input (recommended for older children). When creating rules with children, be sure to change any negative rule to a positive (for example, use "keep your hands to yourself" versus "no hitting" or "inside voices" versus "no yelling").

Be sure to remind the children of the rules/expectations at the beginning of every session and actively identify when children follow the rules. Be sure to offer praise as well for following rules and expectations. You will also want to be clear about consequences if children do not meet the group expectations.

For instance, sample rules may be:
- Be on time and prepared for the session
- Be respectful by listening and quiet while others are talking
- Stay on your own mat
- Be supportive of everyone
- Be willing to try everything
- Use kind words
- Have fun

# V. Information for Facilitators: Communication Skills

## Compassionate Communication

As a facilitator, your most important skill will be communication. Compassionate communication means communicating in a way that shows care by truly listening and builds understanding by acknowledging what you heard the other person say. When we understand each other, group sessions will run more smoothly and children will get the most out of their group experience. Children learn from the people around them, so the way you communicate with the children in your classes will be teaching children how they are expected to communicate with others. Modeling (showing) compassionate communication reinforces and encourages positive, clear and kind interactions between children.

> *Ask yourself:*
> - When I think about communication, what comes to mind as being important for clear, effective communication? Think about the last communication I had that felt clear, supportive and helpful—what made it successful?
> - What are some things that get in the way of good communication? Think about the last time a communication went badly for me—what went wrong?
> - Where did I learn my communication style? Think about the people I know who model good communication. How have they influenced me?

## Active Listening and Mirroring

What to say and how to say it are important aspects of communication, but another equally important aspect for facilitators to be aware of is listening. There are many different ways of listening. When listening to music or to the radio, you may do it without thinking and sometimes you can even forget what you've heard, almost as if you weren't really listening at all. Active listening, on the other hand, means paying attention and checking to make sure that you are taking in and understanding what you are hearing. This type of listening builds good communication. When you are communicating with children, listening is as important as speaking.

Communication happens in many ways—you communicate nonverbally through behavior and verbally through words. When you are listening actively, physical and verbal actions communicate your interest and understanding. For example, posture, eye contact, and facial expressions communicate a lot! These physical communicators are as important when listening to a message, as they are when we're sharing one. Matching children's body language and expression often communicates that you understand what they're feeling and are on the same wavelength. You can also express this through nodding and other common expressions of attention. Matching or mirroring can help people feel understood, and can also help children to better understand themselves by seeing their own experience being reflected by someone else. Mirroring can also be verbal. Mirroring out loud through active listening includes these techniques: reflecting, paraphrasing, assessing and exploring.

- When you use reflecting, you listen carefully and remember what the person says in order to say aloud what is going on and what the person may be feeling.
- Paraphrasing is a way of restating what the person has said to show you understand. You can do this by rewording what was said, or putting their words into your own words to check if you've understood them correctly. For example saying, "I hear you saying...," or "it sounds like..."
- You probably do a lot of assessing and exploring in communication with others. When doing this, you ask questions to clarify what was said and encourage further expression. You might say "that must have made you feel...", ask if you've understood correctly, or ask if they could share more to help you understand better.

When asking questions, open-ended questions (instead of yes/no questions) help in building understanding. Open ended questions encourage a child to explain in their own way. These questions might start with, "tell me more about," "or "I heard you say __, what did you mean?" Try to avoid questions with yes/no answers when mirroring. Asking "why" may be confusing or frustrating for some children if they don't know the answer. When we ask for further clarification, we often learn the "why" through a natural process of elaborating.

> **Ask yourself:**
> - The next time I have a conversation, I will try to express interest and understanding using only words for a moment or two (no non-verbal communication) and ask myself, How did I do that? Did the other person seem to understand that I'm listening?
> - Remember the last time I felt really listened to—what sorts of things did people say or do to help me feel understood? Can I identify any types of mirroring that the listener was using?

## Non-Judgmental Communication

As a facilitator, be accepting and non-judgmental so that children can feel comfortable sharing in the group. You can communicate that you are non-judgmental by making sure your communication is truthful and descriptive and based in fact, rather than based in assumptions or personal thoughts and beliefs.

Non-judgmental communication asks for what you want, instead of saying what you don't want or saying a behavior as bad. For example, instead of saying "don't do that," ask for what you would like the children to do. When you ask for behavior in a positive way, children will feel less shamed, blamed or defensive and will be better able to hear and respond to what you're asking. Again, instead of saying "don't yell," you might say, "please use quiet voices;" instead of saying "no running," try "please walk;" instead of saying "no name calling," say "treat other children with respect."

## Non-violent communication

Violence and non-violence can be communicated both with words and actions. Aggressive or violent communication, whether expressed through an unkind word, a shove, or the silent treatment, can make it hard for children to feel safe in group sessions. As a facilitator, be sure you're communicating safety with your words and your actions including hand gestures, tone of voice, phrases, or even body posture.

When working with children who have experienced trauma of any kind, we need to be extra careful and thoughtful regarding our own behavior. Sometimes when facilitators express frustration, children may misinterpret that frustration as anger, aggression, hatred, rage, or violence directed towards them. Make sure to talk about these issues when they happen—either in your group or one-on-one with children you are worried about. If you are frustrated and find yourself raising your voice or gesturing aggressively in some way during a group, it will be important to notice, mention, name this, take responsibility, and re-establish safety with the group. One way to take responsibility is to apologize, which can be helpful and important for children to experience and then model from.

# Communicating with Children

As children grow and change in age and ability, so do their needs, interests and ways of learning. Children learn best when adults communicate with them using language they understand and concepts that are geared to their age and stage of development. Each age group has specific strengths and interests that can help teachers make age-appropriate choices in selecting stories, characters and words to use. Keeping communication creative and playful can help kids stay engaged in their learning.

Always strive for involving children actively (also called interactive communication) by asking questions and listening to the responses and encouraging children to ask questions and listen to each other. When children are invited to actively participate in conversation, they are more likely to focus and enjoy their experience. Interactive communication provides children and adolescents the opportunity to be fully engaged with what they are learning.

The following guidelines might be helpful when planning your lessons with children:
*   For children from birth through 6 years old, repetition, rhythm, and song can be really helpful. Children in this age group think and learn through images and enjoy stories with human and animal characters. Pictures and hand gestures help learning for this age group. Rhymes, riddles, tongue twisters, and simple jokes may also help keep young children engaged.
*   For children 7 through 10 years old, use stories similar to their lives and experiences to help children understand their worlds. Try using stories about friendships, new skills or talents, and daily experiences.
*   For adolescents 11 through 14 years, use positive role models to help kids form their own sense of right and wrong, their morals and values. Use stories about how family and friends might influence our thoughts, feelings, and beliefs. Avoid giving lectures. Encourage young adolescents to explore and experiment with independence in the presence of safe adults—like you! All kids learn best when adults communicate with them using language they understand and concepts that are geared to their age and stage of development. Each age group has specific strengths and interests that can help teachers make age-appropriate choices in selecting stories, characters, and words to use. Keeping communication creative and playful can help kids stay engaged in their learning.

*Ask yourself:*
*   Think about the age range of the children I work with. What have I noticed that helps them stay engaged?
*   Think about a positive experience I have had working with the children in my setting. What did I learn from that experience that I'd like to include in my lessons?
*   What else would I add to this list from my own experience working with children in my setting?

## Communicating Across Cultures

Cultures offer people ways of thinking, seeing, hearing, and interpreting the world. The way language is used varies between cultures, even when cultures speak the same language. When you are not familiar with cultural differences, there is a greater possibility of miscommunication. Learning about these differences helps to improve communication.

The culture in which you are raised influences your attitudes, beliefs, values and behaviors.  Your "culture" might be influenced by experiences in your families, schools, religious institutions, living situations, communities, and through exposure to the media among others.

> *Ask yourself:*
> - What attitudes, beliefs, and values are most important to me? How did those become so important to me? Where did I learn them?
> - What do I identify as my "cultural background?" What makes up the important parts of my cultural identity?

Cultural sensitivity is being aware of, and accepting of, other cultures and their ways of doing things, even if it's different than what you're used to. Being culturally sensitive means trying not to place your own cultural judgments, thoughts, feelings, beliefs, and perspectives on others' behaviors. Remember, behaviors can have different meanings from culture to culture, or place to place. For example, something that is rude in one culture might be a sign of respect in another culture.

> *Ask yourself:*
> - Thinking about experiences I've had with people from different cultures, what differences stood out? How did I work to understand these differences? What helped me understand them?
> - Have I ever said or done something that was misunderstood because of a cultural difference? What was said or done to help come to a shared understanding?
> - What are cultural traits, beliefs, or behaviors that come to mind when I think about the culture of the children I am working with?

# VI. Information for Facilitators: Boundaries and Consistency

## Healthy boundaries

*Ask yourself:*
- Think about my comfort level and style. What helps me feel safe and comfortable with others?
- Are there people I feel more or less comfortable around? Think about what helps me feel comfortable and what makes me uncomfortable.
- Has this changed at all since I was a child?

When working with at-risk-youth who may have experienced trauma it is important to think about physical and emotional boundaries.

Boundaries are the lines we draw around ourselves to feel safe. Boundaries can be spoken about or unspoken, and help give us a protective distance from someone else's body, words or energy (Street Yoga, 2012). While personal boundaries differ for each person, they serve to help us determine how much information about ourselves we want to share, and the level of physical distance we need in order to feel safe.

At-risk youth may not have developed healthy boundaries for themselves. For example, some youth who may have experienced trauma or abuse that violated (or crossed) boundaries may leave them unclear about what healthy boundaries are.

Having unclear boundaries or crossing boundaries may be triggering for trauma survivors. When children are triggered they may behave in extreme ways or may emotionally shut-down. Because of this, it is important to have a clear policy about boundaries as well as effectively communicate that policy to everyone involved in the group sessions.

## Physical boundaries

When working with children who may have experienced trauma, a "no-touch" policy is recommended. When touch seems necessary, always ask permission to touch and have group members ask each other for permission also. Be sure to allow children to agree to or decline to being touched, and respect their decision. If you are given permission to use touch, try to speak your actions aloud to the person as you proceed, so that what you are doing is clear. This helps touch be less confusing or threatening, and makes it less likely to trigger (dysregulate) a child or to be misunderstood. It is important also to think about how close to someone you are sitting or standing and when working with a child who is easily triggered you may want to ask permission even to step or sit closer.

Sometimes it is challenging not to use touch in group sessions because teaching may be made easier through a physical adjustment or offering physical support. In other cases, it may feel challenging because you want to express care for another person. In either case, consider how you can use your words or think creatively to express that wish, care or support without touch. If touch is used in a session, make sure at least two adults are facilitating the session to ensure safety of the children and the adults.

## Emotional boundaries

Trauma survivors and at-risk-youth sometimes have difficulty with social and emotional boundaries. Some children may be quick to share personal stories (some of which may not be appropriate), while others may be hesitant to trust others and keep their distance.

As a facilitator, it will be important to reflect on your own boundaries. We all have experienced times when it is either easy or difficult to set boundaries.  Pay careful attention to your interactions with the children in your groups. Sometimes you might want to help the children you work with beyond your role as group facilitator. This may come from a place of compassion and wanting to help, but might cause boundaries to get crossed. Before acting on an impulse to help, ask yourself  "Would I behave this way for each and every member of the group? Is it fair to the rest of the group to do ___ for this child? Is this an action that models good boundaries to the participants?'

Because boundaries can be complicated and are so important, it is a good idea to clarify your role, and the boundaries of that role, before beginning the group.  Take time to reflect on the following questions:

> ### Ask yourself:
> * What do I think my role should be in this group?
> * What is reasonable to expect of myself? What is manageable to take on?
> * What would feel unmanageable and unreasonable?
> * Why do I want to do this work? How can I balance my desire to help with the boundaries of my role?

You may notice a desire to go above-and-beyond for the children you work with, but it may or may not be possible to do for long periods of time without getting "burnt-out". Also children might interpret this sort of desire to help in many different ways. On the one hand, children may feel special to have someone who cares about them. On the other hand, it might feel scary for children to have someone care so much for them.  This is especially true for children who have had inconsistent, neglectful, or abusive caregivers. When caregivers give too much and then get burnt-out and withdraw, children can feel abandoned and lose trust. This is just one possible consequence but is important keep in mind as you figure out appropriate boundaries for yourself.

## Communicating About Boundaries

Once you are clear about your role and your boundaries in the group, make your boundaries known to the children through your words and your behaviors. One way to do this is simply to discuss your role with your group at the beginning of the group sessions. For facilitators who also work in residential programs where children live, facilitating the group adds a new role to your relationship with the children, and it will be important to describe the different roles and set boundaries. For example, you can start a group with a simple, straightforward age-appropriate announcement, such as, for older children, "I'm [your name], and many of you might know me because I'm a staff member here, and I've worked with you in that role. For this group time, however, I'm going to be helping you with learning more about yourself and your feelings, relationships, experiences, and plans for the future. I'm also going to help you to understand that you always have a choice and that you are in control of your body. We will meet for [number of] sessions, and each session will be one hour long. Sessions will be [state the frequency of meetings] and will begin at [start time] and end at [ending time]. During this time, I'll be happy to help you understand your feelings and experiences, to the best of my ability, and in a way that will be helpful for you and your group mates. My role here is a little different than you may be used to, and for some of you it might feel strange that our roles are a little different, or maybe it will feel strange to interact differently when we are not in this group. Our group is a space where you can share those feelings if they come arise, and we can talk about them."

*Ask yourself:*
- In my setting, and with the children I work with, what should I communicate about my role and boundaries?
- What questions may children have?
- What questions do I have about possible dual roles at my site?

## The Importance of Consistency

Children come to understand the world through experiences with other people—especially the people who take care of them. By interacting with others, children form meanings about themselves and others, what to expect from others, how to relate to them and how the world works. For children who had adverse, chaotic, or traumatic experiences, they learn that the world can be unsafe, and that people sometimes act in unfair, unsafe, and unpredictable ways. They might also believe that they are responsible for bad things that happened to them. Children are never responsible for abuse from adults. Some children respond to feeling powerless and helpless during abuse by later feeling that they need to control others and the world around them. In these cases, children take on responsibilities far beyond what is healthy for children (Blaustein & Kinniburgh, 2010).

As a caregiver or facilitator, you can help repair unhealthy ideas children form about their world due to early abuse and neglect. One way to do this is by providing a safe environment as an alternative to the chaos and unsafety of their trauma. Part of building a safe environment for children is being consistent and predictable. These are building blocks for safety. Providing consistent rules, expectations, and routines helps children to know what to expect next. Consistent limits with balanced praise and consequences allow children to learn that they can trust adults to support their growth, and show that they are important and deserving to be cared for. Having responsible rules and boundaries (not having to guess) helps children feel safe enough to relax, form relationships with others and begin to explore and play.

**Ask yourself:**
- In my own life, how has consistency and understanding rules and boundaries been helpful to me?
- Are there ways that consistency and routine is already in place for some of the children I work with? How can I build on that?
- Have the children I work with experienced competent caregivers earlier in their lives who have been consistent, set clear rules and expectations, or had the time or energy to follow through on them? How do I think this influences their experiences today?

## Losses and Transitions

It is helpful if all children and facilitators who begin the group remain for the entire program (covering 12 lesson topic areas) so that the group remains predictable and consistent. However, this may not be possible. Group members and facilitators may be absent temporarily due to illness or other circumstances that keep them away. They may end up being absent permanently because they've moved to a different home, have returned to their families, or have prolonged illness.

Throughout the group sessions, children will bond with one another and the facilitators, and become attached. This bonding and attachment is welcome and encouraged. Some groups end up feeling like family, some like close friends, or others simply work and play together. For some children, your group may be the first place where they have felt safe. Since groups can be powerful, a loss (or losses) in the group, whether temporary or permanent, can have a big impact on children.

Many children in your group may have experienced loss and transition that they were not prepared for, and may not have had the opportunity to deal with or recover from. When previous losses are not discussed, new losses may reactivate the strong feelings that were not dealt with before. Group losses may trigger old losses and sad feelings, or even trauma reactions.

Children may feel a sense of loss and grief, or even anger at the absent group member; or sometimes might feel responsible for the absence of a group member. Alternately, children may feel concerned, worried, or fearful for the group member who is absent. Group losses and absences are experienced in a many ways, are important to notice, recognize and talk through together as a group.

**Ask yourself:**
- Thinking about the children at the site where I am working, what have I learned their experience has been with loss?
- How have they dealt with loss in the past? What has helped them to cope?
- How have I dealt with losses, or big changes or transitions in my life?

## Implications for Class

All groups may experience losses and transitions that are unexpected. Because of this, when you anticipate an upcoming disruption or know that a transition is coming, it is best to talk about it and remind the children or youth that it's coming. For example, you will want to share with the group if you know in advance you will be absent for group sessions or if a group is not able to meet due to a holiday or other expected interruptions in the regular schedule. Group members should have an opportunity to announce in group if they know in advance that they will be absent. Also, at the end of group, announcements of disruptions should be repeated or noted. If a group member is unexpectedly absent, mention that to the group. This framework—of beginning and ending group by helping participants prepare for what is to come—creates a holding environment where children are given the time, opportunity, and consideration of preparing for upcoming changes.

If someone has to leave the group permanently, you will want to make an opportunity for children to create a means to say goodbye to the child and thank them for being part of the group. This might be as simple as each group member sharing something with the person who is leaving. Or, this could involve making a group card or poster as a memory from the group. There are many possibilities for this. As a facilitator, be creative and encourage group ideas to find the activity that feels right for the group and its members. Whatever the method, it is important to recognize, and acknowledge the change. If a change is unexpected, you can create a similar process for the remaining members even if the missing group member can be present.

*Ask yourself:*
- Can I think of a time you experienced a loss or change? How did I acknowledge that?
- What was or could have been helpful about using a ritual to mark that change?
- What sort of transitions or losses can I anticipate for my group?
- For the children I'm working with, would talking about transitions be of most help? Or are there specific activities or routines that come to mind that would work best for these children?

# VII. Information for Facilitators: Behavior Management

*Ask yourself:*
- What kinds of behavior difficulties have I noticed among the children I work with?
- When I think about behaviors I have seen that are difficult to manage, what comes to mind? Are they age-appropriate? What do others think about these behaviors? Is there a difference between a child's behavior and who the child is?
- What does it mean if a child I'm working with is "acting up" or "acting out" in a group session? What might the child be trying to tell me with their behavior? Try to determine what he or she is trying to communicate...

In any new situation or group, it is normal and expected for children to test boundaries and behavior. They do this to learn what is appropriate or inappropriate, tolerable or not tolerable. Expecting challenging behaviors and learning how to respond when children test limits is one of the best ways to avoid difficulties and ensure a successful class. Sometimes testing limits may include the following behaviors:

- Fidgeting
- Talking to peers
- Speaking out of turn
- Using "inappropriate language"
- Not responding/ignoring others
- Being in people's physical space
- Not following directions
- Laughing inappropriately
- Being disrespectful to peers or group facilitators

However please note and understand that these behaviors may not always represent testing limits but instead may be signs of an inability to self-regulate without the implied negative connotation of limit-testing. Instead of looking at the behavior as a challenging negative one, it may be helpful for the facilitator to step back and think about the motivation behind the behavior. Could it be that the child is highly agitated, or aroused or even withdrawn due to past experiences? If this seems likely time and understanding might be more beneficial than consequences.

As a facilitator, think about what needs to be communicated to help children know what is appropriate. It is important to be clear about what to expect, how the session will be run, and what is expected of the children. By doing this, and establishing safe routines children may know what is expected of them without having to "act out".

Children are more likely to act out or test limits when they are bored, distracted, or not actively engaged. Forming a strong relationship and actively engaging each child in your group is a helpful way to prevent behavior problems from appearing.

When behavior problems arise, and they will, be sure to address them as soon as possible in a respectful and predictable way. When behavior problems are mild, simply redirect the child to return to the group activity through a clear instruction or reminder about what they should be doing. Be sure to ask for the behavior you want instead of focusing on what you don't want. Acknowledge the positive behaviors of students who are doing what is expected of them. This positive reinforcement of the behaviors you want to see often helps children notice their own disruptive behaviors and correct them.

When a child's behaviors are more problematic or disruptive, and the child doesn't respond to being redirected, ask the supporting facilitator (or co-facilitator) to intervene individually with the child. Effective behavior management might include helping a child manage their behavior one-on-one, or giving them a clear choice of how to re-join the group (for example, if a child is off away from his/her mat ask if he/she would prefer to hop to the mat or skip to the mat; give a choice of yoga poses to practice- "You can do this pose or that pose, the choice is up to you or "you can sit in the relaxing spot and come back when you are ready, or we can walk back together."). If a behavior is truly disruptive and unmanageable, you might find it necessary for the child (with an assistant) to take time away from the group to calm down. You can also ask the child directly what they think would help solve the problem.

**The Safe Place**
The Safe Place was developed by Dr. Becky Bailey as part of her Conscious Discipline® program for behavior management in school classrooms. It has been an effective tool in the **reachwithin** sessions when set up and used properly.

What is the Safe Place?
The Safe Place provides an opportunity for children to remove themselves from the group when upset, angry or frustrated in order to regain composure and self-regulation when upset, angry or frustrated. Children come to the Safe Place in order to be helpful and not hurtful to themselves and others. Since the Safe Place is set up in the same room where the sessions are being held, children are still able to observe and absorb what is happening in their session, while under observation of the facilitator.

How to set up the Safe Place:
- Identify a comfortable area set off to the side of the main teaching area
- Label the area the Safe Place with a sign
- Create a board with visuals incorporating the 5 steps of Self Regulation:
  1) I Am ..... going to/in the Safe Place
  2) I Can Calm .... pictures of a star, drain, pretzel, balloon,
  3) I Feel...... pictures of faces, angry, sad, bored, happy, scared etc
  4) I Choose ..... options of calming activities to choose from eg. Squeezing a soft ball, journaling, writing in the 'angry book', coloring, hugging a stuffed animal, rubbing on 'cranky cream'
  5) I Solve..... problem solving that may need teacher intervention after session
- The area should be a comfortable area for sitting (e.g. cushions, beanbags, yoga mats) with calming items that are appropriate for the age group (e.g. stuffed toys, notepad and pencils, crayons, squeeze balls, reading books)

- Work together with the session in order to establish the Safe Place rules. You may need to prompt them with questions such as: Who can use the Safe Place? Why do we use the Safe Place? How long can one person stay there? What if two people want to be in the Safe Place at the same time? Ensure that the group agrees on a set of rules. Discuss with children rules for returning to the group after being in the Safe Place.
- Write the rules on poster board and keep them in the Safe Place.

Safe Place Props:
Design a Safe Place card. This card can be given to the child by the facilitator as permission to go to the Safe Place, or the facilitator may use it as a suggestion that it might be helpful if the child goes to the Safe Place.

Things to keep in mind:
- The Safe Place should be introduced and set up in the beginning of the program or during one of the initial sessions.
- The Safe Place must not be seen as punishment or time out.
- Rather than simply sending a child to the Safe Place, it is important that you offer the child two choices, one of which is the Safe Place. The facilitator can say " I can see you're getting upset—would you like to leave the group, go to the Safe Place or stay on your mat and join in?"
- Do not expect a child who is upset to change their behavior immediately upon entering the Safe Place. As long as the child's behavior in the Safe Place is not too disruptive to the session, he/she can be allowed to act out until his/her emotions are regulated.
- The child should be guided (with the assistant facilitator) to work through the Safe Place.
- The main facilitator should invite the child back to the class at regular intervals, once they seem calm and regulated.

> **Ask yourself:**
> - Thinking back to times I was in a group as a child (or a recent experience I've had), what helped me to focus, pay attention or participate?
> - What might have helped me be more active in the group or deepen my experience?
> - How did the group facilitator help others who were struggling in the group? What did I notice worked best for me or the other kids during difficult moments?
> - Thinking about the group I will be working with, what challenging behaviors from children am I most concerned about? How can I be prepared to manage these?

Here are a few extra tips from past facilitators about preventing behavioral difficulties:

- Learn and use the children's names to show that you care about them
- Identify children in the group who demonstrate leadership skills and engage them to involve the other youth
- For children who tend to be disruptive together, have them sit farther away from each other
- Remind the children of the group rules/expectations at the start of every session
- Keep instructions simple and straight-forward.
- Find creative ways to actively engage the children; this might include having children help demonstrate activities, help with tasks, or even teach an activity.

Don't feel like you have to intervene for every behavioral difficulty. Have some sense of what may represent crossing the line for you or for other members of the group. It is most important to respond to behaviors that are dangerous or make others feel unsafe. Otherwise, it is your choice to intervene or choose not to.

> **Ask yourself:**
> - What behaviors or challenges would you consider unacceptable?
> - Which behaviors do I imagine would be helpful to let go of if they are not posing a problem to other members' safety or well being?

## What to expect in terms of children's development

Children's behaviors depend a lot on where children are in terms of their development. Knowing some basic information about child development can help you best support the children you work with and address challenges.

As children grow, their brains, bodies, and personalities go through many changes. What a child is able to do and the way he or she thinks at one age may be very different from their abilities at another age.

Children develop in many different ways—physically (in terms of body growth and physical ability), mentally (in terms of thinking and understanding), and emotionally (in terms of feeling and forming relationships).

There are "typical" developmental stages in children's growth to expect, but not every child will experience these stages in the same way or at the same time depending on their past experiences.  In fact, sometimes as children get ready to face a big developmental change, their growth might seem to stop or regress. You can think of this as resting to get ready for the big change, or gearing up to leap forward. It is important to be patient with children as they are constantly growing and changing, which can be hard work.

Below, you will find information about children of different age ranges and what you can expect for their physical, mental and emotional growth. Be sure to read about and reflect on the information for the specific age group of children you work with. These descriptions reflect "normal" development where there has not been a great deal of adversity or hardship. It is important to understand how "normal" development progresses in order to recognize that atypical development can be the result of abuse, trauma, neglect and/or maltreatment. These negative experiences often make children develop in a way that does not appear to be age appropriate. Children who have experienced trauma may not meet expected levels of cognitive and social skills; may have difficulty with self-regulation and may not have had the chance to develop healthy boundaries. Additionally, they may always be on "alert", which can then interfere with their ability to focus, concentrate, and interact in an age-appropriate manner. They may also have trouble understanding their feelings as well as those of others.

### Infants

Most infants (0-12 months) are interested in people and in toys. At this age they notice cause and effect. For example, they might notice that if they drop their favorite toy it makes a noise when it hits the floor. Infants aren't able to talk, so they show feelings and needs through crying, facial expressions, and body movement. Caregivers learn to read these cues to help comfort infants when they are upset. Infants begin to grow emotionally by being comforted when they are upset. Physically, infants grow quickly. In the beginning they are not strong enough to control their movements, but over the first twelve months become able to support their own heads and eventually sit up, stand and walk with the support of an adult.

> **Ask yourself:**
> * Think about a child I know who's in this age range I am working with.
> * What are they like in terms of abilities and interests?
> * What else comes to mind when I think about the strengths and challenges for children of this age in my setting, location, or culture?
> * What things are they focused on at this age?
> * What comes to mind about different ways I can help and support them?

### Young Children

In terms of cognitive development, children ages one through five are curious about the world and will want to see how things work. During these years they learn language and speaking—first a few words (around age one), and then complete sentences (around age five). By age five, they may count up to 20 and do simple subtraction. In terms of emotional development, young children are usually very connected to their caregivers. Starting at one year old, children begin to recognize their own emotions and start to learn how to manage them. However, they will need adults to comfort them and help them work through difficult feelings and experiences. They will not fully recognize emotions in others and will not be able to understand the cause of others' feelings until later. By the time they are five years old, they often start trying to work through their feelings by themselves. One to three year olds will play near, but usually not with, other children.  By age five, they may be more excited about group play.  Physically, around two years of age (about 20 months old) many children will go from crawling to walking to running. When they reach age five, they will be able to play for long periods of time.  Two and three year olds mostly scribble, but five-year-olds often have enough finger control to learn to write.

*Ask yourself:*
- Think about a child I know who's in this age range I am working with.
- What are they like in terms of abilities and interests?
- What else comes to mind when I think about the strengths and challenges for children of this age in my setting, location, or culture?
- What things are they focused on at this age?
- What comes to mind about different ways I can help and support them?

## Later Childhood

In middle childhood, children ages six-12 years old pay attention for longer periods of time and tend to like activities that are planned and structured, like games with rules.  Children begin to read and gain skills in reading. Emotionally, six-12 year olds become better able to handle some feelings on their own, and may be proud of that. At this age, children will still need and sometimes ask for adult help with tough experiences, feelings and relationships. Being able to count on routines help children at this age know what to expect and feel safe. By eight years old many children will develop some coping strategies for stressful situations, and as they understand the idea of covering up their feelings they will sometimes try this out. Physically, kids in middle childhood gain coordination for big and small activities, like swinging a baseball bat or holding a pencil and writing. More physical activity will help develop these physical skills more quickly.  Dance, sports and yoga can improve coordination and strength.

*Ask yourself:*
- Think about a child I know who's in this age range I am working with.
- What are they like in terms of abilities and interests?
- What else comes to mind when I think about the strengths and challenges for children of this age in my setting, location, or culture?
- What things are they focused on at this age?
- What comes to mind about different ways I can help and support them?

## Adolescence

Adolescents ages 13-18 will grow taller and gain strength. The biggest physical change in adolescence is sexual maturation, also called puberty. Adolescents are also beginning to figure out their own identity. It takes time for adolescents and their caregivers to understand and get to know these new identities and new bodies. Remember that not all children develop in the same way or at the same rate—especially during adolescence. It is normal for adolescents to wonder whether they are "normal" and may feel self-conscious about their bodies. Cognitively, adolescents start to use logical thinking to figure out answers to problems, and also begin to think broadly about concepts and theories. Adolescents often compare ideas and start to be able to make multi-step plans. Over time, adolescents become more self-reflective and question morals, values and behavior. Emotionally, as children grow into teenagers they become better at working through their feelings on their own (in healthy situations). When they need help with feelings and relationships they often ask friends before talking to adults. Under stress, adolescents may behave in childish ways. Teen years are an exciting time, but it can also be very stressful and full of complicated feelings. Younger adolescents will not think much about the future; older adolescents may think a lot about their plans for their future.

*Ask yourself:*
- Think about a child I know who's in this age range I am working with.
- What are they like in terms of abilities and interests?
- What else comes to mind when I think about the strengths and challenges for children of this age in my setting, location, or culture?
- What things are they focused on at this age?
- What comes to mind about different ways I can help and support them?

# VIII. Self-Care and Stress

Working with children is incredibly meaningful, fulfilling, and fun, but at the same time can be stressful. Many children you will work with have suffered and struggled through various adversities including various types of emotional difficulties. Some may have lost loved ones, others may have been neglected, abused, witnessed or experienced community violence, or lived in poverty. As a facilitator, this work may impact you in unexpected ways. Some people feel energized by the work, and some people find themselves exhausted. One way to keep from becoming overwhelmed is to make sure you are taking care of yourself.

## Developing a Self-Care Plan

It is important to have specific ideas of how to care for yourself. One way is to develop a self-care plan and check-in with yourself each week regarding self-care and checking for warning signs of vicarious stress and vicarious trauma. A self-care plan can be as simple as writing down the ways you take care of yourself, things you enjoy, and what makes you feel better. Ask yourself the following questions:

- What do I do to take care of myself physically?
- What do I do to take care of myself psychologically?
- What do I do to take care of myself emotionally?
- What do I do to take care of myself spiritually?

*Ask yourself:*
- Think back to times I felt fatigued, burnt out, stressed, or triggered. What happened in those situations? What helped me get through those difficult times?
- How will I respond if I feel stressed, burnt out, fatigued, or triggered in the future? What can I plan on for self-care to help prevent or cope with those responses?
- Create a list of self-care activities you could use in a moment's notice. These self-care activities could take 5 minutes, 10 minutes, 30 minutes, an hour and more.
- How can I create both short-term and long-term self-care goals for myself? How many self-care strategies do I want to use each week? What two self-care activities that take the most time can I challenge myself to this week?

The more self-care possibilities you give yourself, the more likely it will be for you to put your self-care plan into action. And, the more you take care of yourself, the less likely you are to experience vicarious stress or trauma. This self-care strategy will allow you to be a great model for the children, which will in turn allow you to feel more available to do this important work.

## Vicarious Stress and Vicarious Trauma

While working with children who have faced difficult and traumatic situations, you might experience unexpected changes in yourself. Some common experiences include changes in the following areas: how you view the world around you, feeling hopeless or helpless, feeling like you can't do enough, feeling scared, changing how you are in relationship to others, feeling distracted, having low motivation and feeling detached or numb from your work, yourself, or your relationships. Reactivation of old personal trauma or emotional upsets may resurface. Sometimes these experiences are called vicarious stress, vicarious traumatization, compassion fatigue, empathic strain, or burnout. When people witness trauma or stressful events of others over time, it is common to take on those experiences, or begin to feel them ourselves. "Vicarious stress" is manifested differently in each person.

**In order to take good care of yourself, be on the lookout for the following important signs:**
- Changes in your feelings about yourself, the world, or your spirituality
- Feeling angry and cynical
- Feeling more sensitive than usual
- Feeling uncharacteristically desensitized or minimizing of traumatic, stressful or violent events or stories
- Experiencing bystander guilt, or an unusually heavy wish that you could have done something to stop or alter your students' experiences
- Feeling numb and unable to empathize with others
- Feeling rage, dread, horror, shame or grief
- Finding it difficult to listen to others and avoiding interactions
- Experiencing increased self-criticism
- Feeling chronically exhausted
- Changes in the way you relate to important people in your life—are you pulling away or needing more attention than usual?
- Experiencing posttraumatic symptoms, such as nightmares, intrusive images of the stories you've heard or experiences you've witnessed, or fearful, hyper vigilant and avoidant behaviors
- Feeling demoralized and wanting to quit your job
- Feeling like you can never do enough
- Wanting to be alone and avoiding experiences where you have to interact with others, including close friends and family members

## How to protect yourself from vicarious trauma

There are a number of things that can be done in addition to self-care in order to protect yourself from vicarious traumatization.

**Awareness:** The first step is to anticipate and raise your own awareness about the possibility of vicarious stress and vicarious trauma. Know what the warning signs are for you that you're feeling overwhelmed.

**Balance:** The next step is to pay attention to balance; it is easier to become overwhelmed or at risk for vicarious stress and vicarious trauma when your life becomes unbalanced. Think about what the right balance is for you between work, play, and rest. Is there a certain amount of social connection that you need? Physical activity? Alone time? Spiritual connection? What helps you maintain and sustain a balanced body, mind, and soul? How can you create that during your time facilitating the group?

***Connection:*** You can also protect against becoming overwhelmed by connecting with others. Because stress and trauma often lead to disconnecting and isolating, the more you connect with other people, the easier it will be to handle potentially overwhelming feelings associated with this work. By connecting with others, you can also gain perspective, step back and see the bigger picture to help one another through the difficulties.

***Rely on your Team:*** Finally, as you begin with this work, remember that the other staff and **reachwithin** representatives are a team. You are there for each other—none of you are in this alone. And because you are a team, you can lean on each other to step in when you need a break, to handle a situation that you feel unable to handle, to brainstorm when you feel stuck, to support you when you feel overwhelmed, and to help add a new perspective when your perspective has narrowed. Make sure you know how to get in touch with your **reachwithin** trainers in the event you feel you need additional support.

> ### Ask yourself:
> - Who are the other people serving the children I work with?
> - Who are the people I feel safe to turn to for support, advice, or fun?
> - How can I support the other members of my team?

## Facilitators' Experiences

Trauma touches everyone's lives in some way. You may have had personal traumatic experiences, or have the experience of being close to others who have experienced traumas. However, everyone has witnessed, through news, television or radio, traumatic events of natural disasters and war.

Because all lives are impacted by trauma, everyone has ways to cope with, and react to these experiences. Memories of some past experiences may be recalled or triggered when working with groups of at-risk youth. Experiencing some triggering is normal. You can prepare yourselves for what might be triggering and plan action steps to take if you become triggered.

## IX. Program Assessment

### Evaluating the progress of the group

Many facilitators find it helpful to use an assessment tool (or questionnaire) to get a sense of how the group members have progressed from the beginning to the end of the **reachwithin** program.

One option is to use a standard assessment tool such as the Strengths and Difficulties Questionnaire (SDQ), which can be downloaded for free at the following website: http://www.sdqinfo.org/. The SDQ website also provides information about the measure, how to use it, and how to interpret the results.

In addition to standardized measures, you can find a questionnaire in this manual that asks specific questions related to the goals of the **reachwithin** program. Please feel free to use the assessment measure on the following pages by completing the questionnaire BOTH before beginning the group and after completing the group. This questionnaire can be used to assess the impact of the group on the children you work with, and can be found as Appendix G later in the manual.

# X. Resources

The following resources may be helpful in your learning about supporting children through skill building, yoga and understanding mental health.

## Yoga Websites

Karmakidsyoga.com

Childrensyoga.com

Yogakids.com

Bentonlearning.com

Littlefloweryoga.com

Yogajournal.com

Specialyoga.com

Buddahfulkids.com

Nextgenerationyoga.com

Trencentral.com

Youthintelligence.com

Buschgardens.com

Yogaed.com

Streetyoga.org

## Books for Teachers

Desikachar, T. K. V. (1995). *The Heart of Yoga*. Rochester, VT: Inner Traditions International

Hahn, T. N. (1975). *The miracle of mindfulness*. Boston, MA: Beacon Press.

Emerson, D., Hopper, E. (2011). *Overcoming trauma through yoga: reclaiming your body*. Berkley, CA: North Atlantic Books.

Lasater, J. (2011). *Relax and renew: Restful yoga for stressful times*. Berkley, CA: Rodmell Press.

Myss, C. (1996). *Anatomy of the sprit: The seven stages of power and healing*. New York, NY: Three Rivers Press.

Rosenberg, M. (2003). *Nonviolent communication: A language of life*. Encinitas, CA: PuddleDancer Press.

Salzberg, S. (1995). *Loving kindness: The revolutionary art of happiness*. Boston, MA: Shambala Publications, Inc.

Salzberg, S. (2008). *Quiet mind: A beginner's guide to meditation*. Boston, MA: Shambala Publications, Inc.

Tolle, E. (1999). *The power of now*. Novato, CA: New World Library.

Wenig, M. (2003). *YogaKids: Educating the whole child through yoga*. New York, NY: Stewart, Tabori and Chang.

## Mental Health and Development Books

– Blaustein, M. E., & Kinniburgh, K. M. (2010). *Treating traumatic stress in children and adolescents*. New York: The Guilford Press.

– Brazelton, T. B. (2006). *Touchpoints*. (2nd ed.). Boston, MA: Da Capo Press.

– Brom, D., Pat-Horenczyk, R., & Ford, J. D. (2009). *Treating traumatized children: Risk, resilience and recovery*. East Sussex: Routledge.

– Gielen, U. & J. Roopnarine (Eds.), *Childhood and Adolescence: Cross-cultural Perspectives and Applications*. Westport, CT: Praeger.

– Heller, L., & Aline, L. (2012). *Healing developmental trauma*. Berkley, CA: North Atlantic Books.Levine,

– P., & Kline, M. (2007). *Trauma through a child's eyes: Awakening the ordinary miracle of healing*. Berkley, CA: North Atlantic Books.Levy, T., & Orlans, M. (1998).

– *Attachment, trauma, and healing*. Washington D. C.: Child Welfare League of America Press.

– Saxe, G. N., Ellis, B. H., & Kaplow, J. B. (2007). *Collaborative treatment of traumatized children and teens*. New York, NY: The Guilford Press.

– Shanker, S. (2013). *Calm, alert, and learning: Classroom strategies for self-regulation*. Toronto: Pearson Canada Inc.Williams, M. B., & Poijula, S. (2002).

– *The PTSD workbook*. Oakley, CA: New Harbinger Publications, Inc.

## Appendix A: Theory Base

### Karma Kids Yoga
Karma Kids Yoga is an instructional program for children to develop strength and flexibility in both mind and body through yoga. Animated poses support strength, coordination, and body awareness, while breathing and visualization techniques support concentration and focus (www.karmakidsyoga.com).

### Street Yoga
Street Yoga teaches yoga, mindful breathing, and compassionate communication to youth and families struggling with homelessness, poverty, abuse, addiction, trauma and other behavioral challenges. It also works with children's caregivers. Street yoga aims to make these children stronger, and work towards healing and creating an inspired, safe, and joyful life (www.streetyoga.org).

### Yoga Ed
The Yoga Ed program comprises of yoga regimens for teachers, parents, children to develop physical fitness, emotional intelligence and stress management to ultimately improve academic achievement. These lessons focus on cultivating self-awareness, self-management and self-care and stress reduction (www.yogaed.com).

### Conscious Discipline
Conscious Discipline integrates classroom management with social-emotional learning, by providing a training program for adults to go through themselves and then implement with children. Conscious Discipline helps adults consciously respond to daily conflict in classrooms, using everyday occurrences as an opportunity to teach critical life skills to children (www.consciousdiscipline.com).

### Trauma Systems Theory
TST is a mental health treatment model, described in a published manual, that helps children and adolescents that have been traumatized by assessing and responding to their emotional and social needs and environment. TST uses many components such as psychotherapy, home-based care and psychopharmacology to help address the symptoms of trauma (www.aboutourkids.org/articles/trauma_systems_therapy_pioneered_dr_glenn_saxe_gains_support_new_research).

### Attachment, Regulation and Competency
ARC stands for the three core domains that are frequently impacted among traumatized youth and which are relevant to future resiliency. ARC is an interventional framework social workers can use to tailor therapy for individuals or groups of youths. ARC is designed for all youth, from early childhood to adolescence, and for their caregivers (www.traumacenter.org/research/ascot.php).

# Appendix B: Developmental Stages Chart

## What to expect in infancy and early childhood:

| Age | Cognitive Development | Emotional Development | Physical Development |
|---|---|---|---|
| 1 | • Very curious, like to repeat experiences<br>• Start using words and even combining them | • Starting to learn to recognize and manage their emotions<br>• Beginning to pretend play, usually by imitating adults | • At around 20 months they go from crawling to running |
| 2 | • Will start asking "why," "what" and "how" questions<br>• They will start to understand concepts like "tomorrow" and "yesterday"<br>• They can sing the ABCs, but will not understand the connection between the sounds and symbols | • They enjoy playing alongside of other children but will keep to themselves<br>• They are starting to recognize emotions in others, when conflicts adults should step in and teach appropriate behaviors | • They are developing their motor skills further, they enjoy dancing upon request, doing finger plays and acting out chants and songs. |
| 3 | • Language in three year olds has taken off<br>• They love hearing stories and understand conversations<br>• They can solve puzzles<br>• They can recognize letters and numbers, can count to 5 | • They need familiar adults to feel comfortable<br>• They begin have to have real friendships with other children<br>• They can manage their emotions but fall apart under stress | • They can start holding writing utensils |
| 4 | • Can count to 10, they can subtract up to 4<br>• They know the days of the week, months, seasons<br>• They cannot yet tell time | • Four-year-olds learn what causes certain feelings and realize that others may react to the same situation differently<br>• Beginning of group play and feeling sympathy | • They are more adept at holding writing utensils<br>• They can play for long periods of time |
| 5 | • 5-year-olds speak grammatically correctly and are greatly expanding their vocabulary<br>• They can count up to 20 and do simple subtraction<br>• They want to learn more about how the world works | • Five-year-olds are more emotionally independent, they may try to resolve their own feelings<br>• Their social skills are improving<br>• They are increasingly concerned with "group" acceptance | • They can move with more coordination (running, swimming, biking with training wheels)<br>• They can manage zippers and buttons |

## What to expect in later childhood and adolescence:

| Age | Cognitive Development | Emotional Development | Physical Development |
|---|---|---|---|
| 6-10 | • These children have longer attention spans and prefer structured activities<br>• They are readers and can enjoy this solitary activity<br>• They capable of counting to 200 at age six. By age ten, they can count to 1000 and multiply and divide numbers<br>• Early in this time imagination and reality may still be linked, (e.g. butterflies with eyelashes) but when the powers of observation are encouraged, these will become separate areas of thought. | • Predictable routines are important for children this age<br>• This age group also gains stability from their interactions with adults with whom they feel secure, particularly during challenging situations and circumstances<br>• They will start to become more independent (and proud of it) but will turn to adults when they need help<br>• By the time they are 8 they will understand masking emotions and will have developed coping strategies for stressful situations | • This is an important age for kids to gain motor skills<br>• Kids who move less will not mature as quickly as kids who dance, play sports, do yoga, etc. |
| 11-13 | • Early adolescent children are increasingly capable of mastering intellectual tasks. However their school grades might go down because this is a period of rebellion<br>• They will begin to use formal logic in schoolwork<br>• They will also begin to question authority<br>• Verbalize opinions and views about things largely relating to his or her own life (friends, sports, etc.) | • Young teens tend to struggle with independence and identity, they can exhibit childish behavior when stressed<br>• Exhibit a tendency not to think much about the future<br>• Focus on making, and greater reliance, on friends<br>• Behavior frequently influenced by peer group<br>• They can be moody<br>• Concerns about being normal | • Beginnings of sexual maturation for both boys and girls<br>• Frequently comes with a big growth spurt, in height and weight |
| 14-16 | • Middle adolescents will think more deeply than they did a few years ago and begin to question their own ethics and behavior, i.e. self-reflection. | • Intense self-involvement<br>• Can be accompanied by poor body-image<br>• Concerns about being normal | • Continued puberty<br>• Girls tend to develop faster than boys |
| 17-18 onwards | • Late adolescents think even more abstractly and morally<br>• May think about the meaning of life | • Continued concerns from middle adolescence<br>• Increased desire for independence | • Continued/completed puberty |

The information on ages 6-10 was compiled from the PBS project, the Child Development Tracker:
http://www.pbs.org/parents/child-development/

The information on adolescence was adapted from American Academy of Child and Adolescent's Facts for Families
eclkc.ohs.acf.hhs.gov/hslc/tta.../_34_Stages_of_adolescence1.pdf

# Appendix C: Facilitator Tips, Dos and Don'ts

**Do...**

*Model Positive Behavior:* **reachwithin** believes that facilitators' most effective way to promote positive behavior in the children is to embody the desired behavior in themselves. This is a powerful and inspirational model. For example, if you are calm and relaxed, you will bring out the same states in the children.

*Use your imagination:* Children have wonderful imaginations, and it can be helpful to include imaginative stories in the group sessions. For example, you can take the children on an imaginary journey through the jungle, and include several yoga poses such as tree pose, cobra pose, lion's pose, etc, as these creatures and natural elements enter your story.

*Challenge* Children need to set goals for difficult poses—many children don't think they can do difficult poses and therefore don't make any effort to practice them. Keep reminding them that they can do anything they set their minds to. Provide constant encouragement so they will continue to work on challenging poses.

*Be kind but firm:* Children and teens will respond well when it is clear that you are the facilitator in the classroom, so it is important to be firm regarding class expectations and rules. However the manner in which you relate to the children should still be kind and respectful. Be calm yet assertive.

*Set the bar high:* Studies have shown that children achieve what is expected of them, so gently challenge the children to go beyond their perceived limits—physical, mental, and emotional. Work with them individually as much as possible to help them work towards their goals.

*Include both routine and spontaneity:* Having regular routines creates structure, safety, and support in the classroom, while spontaneity keeps interest alive and keeps children engaged. Create a solid routine within the group session, but occasionally include a new pose, game, or activity to keep the class exciting.

*Encourage conscious breathing:* Most children and teens are not aware of their breath while practicing yoga poses. Find creative ways to bring their attention to their breath such as counting the breath aloud, breathing together, and using imagery such as balloons for students to conceptualize bringing air in and out fully and deeply.

*Learn to adapt:* Lessons or sequences you have planned may not work on a given day, depending on the mood/energy level of the group. You must have a lot of "tricks" in your bag to pull out at any moment. You also may have to stop the group and have a discussion about respect, motivation, etc., at any given moment, if you think this is necessary to deal with misbehavior or lack of participation.

*Practice Safety:* Give clear instruction in all poses, and, as you teach, keep a close eye to make sure children are practicing safely. Only offer challenging poses when you know a child is strong enough to begin practicing more advanced poses. Be mindful of the language you use: trauma survivors are often very sensitive to what is said, and particularly to how it is said. Trauma sensitive language is concrete and gently brings attention to visceral experiences. Use language of inquiry and invitatory language.

**Be confident in yourself and your teaching:** Children can sense if you are not feeling sure of yourself. Even if your teaching isn't perfect, children rarely notice if you make a mistake. Practice teaching with enthusiasm and confidence. Over time your confidence will grow.

**Be enthusiastic:** Don't be afraid to show your passion for yoga—the more you believe in it and what it can do to transform one's life, the more the children will share your enthusiasm.

**Focus on building strength:** Many children and teens lack physical strength due to their sedentary lifestyles, so it is important to practice a lot of poses that build upper body, core, and leg strength. You can explain to them that these poses are important because they need the strength to be able to do the more advanced poses.

**Be a role model:** Children and teens are very perceptive, so as a group facilitator it is extremely important to embody kindness, gentleness, patience, and compassion in and out of the group.

**Simple Instructions:** Children and teens can sometimes lose interest quickly or have trouble remembering complicated instructions, so it is important to break the poses down into simple, manageable steps.

**Incorporate songs and games:** Use music and sing-along sessions to guide the practice and sustain children's attention throughout the group session. Vary music volume and style depending on the type of poses you plan to teach. For example, switch to a soft song during the final resting pose, or add upbeat tunes during standing poses to emphasize strength and energy.

**Use child-friendly language:** Traditionally, yoga poses have Sanskrit names, which can be confusing for children and teens. Instead of explaining yoga theory to young children, or overwhelming them with words in languages they don't understand, use terms they can understand and remember. Using animal names for poses, such as "Cobra Pose," "Mouse Pose," and "Lion's Pose" makes it easy for children to comprehend. This also provides them with the opportunity to have fun by making their own animal sound effects as they pose, such as barking like a dog in Downward Dog, or hissing like a snake in Cobra Pose.

**Dispel excess energy through activities and games:** Young children often have a great deal of energy that needs to be released in productive ways. Practicing yoga can help young children discharge some of that excess energy, so it is helpful to include games and activities that encourage a great deal of movement.

**Challenge children to move beyond limiting beliefs:** When children become discouraged and say they cannot do a difficult pose, respond with something like "Do the best you can, and it will get easier and better the more you practice". Remind children that what may hold them back most in their yoga practice is not their physical limitations, but their attitude. Challenge children to change their beliefs about what they are capable of—remind them that they have infinite potential—all they need is to believe in themselves as much as you do as their facilitator.

**Encourage a non-judgmental attitude:** While you want to encourage the children to challenge themselves physically, you also want to your children to develop an accepting, non-judgmental attitude of their current abilities. Children will often compare themselves to what others are doing. Ask children to "be on their own mat" and not to worry about what other children are doing. You can tell your children "Yoga is a practice, not a race. There is no right or wrong. You do your best, and that is what counts.", or "Wherever you are in this moment, it is exactly where you need to be". Accepting and honoring where we are today opens the possibility for future growth. You can offer encouragement by saying something like "This was hard for me too but I practiced and it got easier and I got better at it".

**Encourage a more playful attitude towards practicing yoga:** It is helpful for children not to take their yoga practice too seriously. Rather than getting frustrated if they cannot achieve a certain pose right away, they can adopt a more playful attitude by having fun experimenting with difficult poses, therefore removing some of the stress and pressure that comes when trying to master something difficult. If they fall down, no worries! Just as a child gets up after a fall when learning to walk, we also have to get up after a fall from a pose and try again, in a fun and playful way!

**Praise and acknowledge children for what they are doing right:** Many children, especially those who have been traumatized, abused, neglected and/or maltreated, are not accustomed to hearing praise. As their group leader, you may be one of the only positive voices in their lives—and it is a voice they desperately need to hear.

Praise children for what they are doing right, even if it is something that is expected of them, such as being on time, being prepared for the session, or doing a good job participating fully in class. Praise them for even the slightest improvement in their poses or in their behavior. Also praise the children for positive personal skills such as focusing, listening, working well with others, or practicing empathy. Verbal praise is one of the most powerful ways you can build the child's self-confidence and self-esteem.

**Believe in Your Children:** Many children do not believe in themselves, and will not even attempt difficult poses due to fear of failure. Before the children can believe in themselves, you as their facilitator have to believe in them. Encourage them by saying things like "I know this is a difficult pose, but I know you can do it! Try your best every day and in a few months, you will be amazed at what your body is capable of doing." A little encouragement can go a long way.

**Be specific in your praise:** It is easy to give generic praise such as "Beautiful!" "Nice job!" But being more specific with your praise will go a long way and have a much deeper impact on the children. Instead of saying "Great!" "Good work!" say things like, "Your posture has improved so much, Adriana! You carry yourself with pride and you look beautiful holding yourself that way. It's really impressive how you take your yoga practice with you off the mat and integrate it into your life."

**Don't...**

**Be attached to the outcome of your session**: There is a saying, "Do your best and leave the rest." Often as facilitators we have noble intentions of transforming youth through the practices of yoga, and while we may see tremendous growth in some children, you may not see any noticeable changes in others. It is important to not be attached to the outcome of the session—we do not have control over how the practice is received by children. Rather, focus on being the best facilitator you can be. The rest is not in our hands.

**Skip relaxation:** Even young children enjoy and greatly benefit from the deep relaxation period at the end of class. If you are running short on time, be sure to still include relaxation at the end of the session. It is better to leave out a few poses or skip a game than to leave out relaxation.

**Hold poses for too long:** Even the most attentive children can have difficulty staying in one pose for too long so it is important to keep the flow of the class moving and flowing into a range of poses without spending too much time on any given pose.

**Make unpredictable moves:** Stay on your own mat as much as possible to avoid triggering the children in your group.

**Approach a child from behind:** Be mindful that abused or maltreated children are easily triggered by unexpected movements or touch especially from out of their lines of sight.

**Lower your voice to a whisper:** Children who have been sexually abused often have traumatic memories of their perpetrator whispering to them, so avoid whispering to trigger children in your group.

# Appendix D: Accommodating Special Situations

## Pregnancy

Before the first group session it is a good idea to find out if anyone is pregnant. Sometimes girls may be shy or embarrassed and not want to share this news publically (for fear of being singled out). Being mindful of this possibility, ask them in private.

When working with pregnant young women let them know that if something doesn't feel right, it probably isn't. If this is the case, find an adjustment or a modification for the necessary yoga pose(s). If you are not sure how to modify a pose, then always be on the side of caution. Encourage the young pregnant women to stay within their comfort zone and to trust their bodies; their bodies will let them know if a posture or movement feels okay, or if it is too much.

You will also want to keep in mind that pregnancy can bring up a lot of emotions, mood swings, physical discomfort, and confusion, as well as excitement, hope, and joy. It is important to be compassionate and understanding.

## Hints & precautions for teaching pregnant women:

- New to Yoga- If your participant is new to yoga, pregnancy is not a time to learn advanced or inverted postures. The practice at this time is to be mindful and gentle. No forcing or straining.
- Inversions- If experienced with inversions, women can continue practicing during pregnancy with care, support and timely modifications, until it feels right to discontinue. Always be on the side of caution. Remind pregnant women to move slowly. When pregnant women move slowly, they are more mindful of approaching their limits and can therefore appropriately modify or discontinue a posture if and when needed.
- Abdominal exercises/ crunches- After the first trimester, make sure that any posture that contracts their abdominal muscles be avoided.
- Twisting Poses- Encourage practice of open twists. In open twists, the action comes from the back, not from the pelvis. The idea is to lift and extend the spine, making room for the baby. The focus should be on opening the shoulders instead of compressing the abdomen.
- Postures on Belly- Postures on the belly are not recommended after the first trimester.
- Postures on Back- Encourage comfort at all times. Each pregnant woman is unique. Some women feel comfortable to be on their backs at 7 months. Others no longer feel comfortable at 3 months. Placing a rolled towel under the right torso can make postures more comfortable.
- Holding Postures- During pregnancy, many poses become uncomfortable when held for a long time.
- Relaxation Postures- Generally, the most important poses for pregnant women are those that promote relaxation. Side-lying postures can be practiced by lying on their left side, avoiding pressure. Use any props (bolster between legs, blanket under head and belly) to increase comfort. Encourage loving attention to the growing baby inside.
- Cautions- Squatting, deep twists and any uncomfortable poses should be avoided at all times and more careful attention should be pain during the third trimester. Young pregnant women should be encouraged to be aware of changing sensations and to let the facilitator know if there is any pain.

### Injury and common ailments

In teaching yoga, you will often encounter children suffering from various ailments or injuries. The first step in learning how to adapt the yoga practice in order to address various conditions is to learn to distinguish what is a legitimate concern from that of a child looking for an excuse to not participate. Encourage as much participation as possible, and let children know that yoga can help with various ailments and conditions, rather than allowing a child's condition to permit him or her to not participate in the yoga class.

Some children will choose not to participate for various reasons. Rather than stopping the whole class and trying to force a child to participate, quietly approach the child and ask why they are not participating. If the child is not cooperating, it is best to just let them be. Have a conversation with the child after class about why they did not participate to determine what the underlying issue is. Try to understand the reasons behind what may have led to their withdrawal.

### Complaining

Children often have a myriad of excuses as to why they can't participate. Common complaints include: being tired, having menstrual cramps, not feeling well, being upset over a situation, a certain body part hurting, etc. It is your job as the facilitator to make a distinction between a valid complaint from an excuse not to participate. Decisions should be made on an individual basis. However unless children are clearly unwell or injured, generally encourage them to do as much as they can. Reinforce the idea that yoga most often helps common ailments such as cramps and fatigue. For example, if a student complains of being tired, encourage the child to practice sun salutations and backbends, as they both increase energy.

### Back Pain

One of the most common ailments among youth is back pain. Yoga is incredibly therapeutic for treating back pain, and helps to both stretch and strengthen the core muscles and back muscles that support the spine. See poses in Appendix F recommended for treating back pain.

### Poses and breathing practices for common ailments

Deep breathing and deep relaxation help to boost the immune system and can lessen the severity of a wide variety of ailments and conditions. Regardless of the specific injury or condition at hand, breathing and relaxation should always be included as a tool for healing. In addition to deep relaxation and deep breathing, see Appendix F for specific poses and breathing exercises that may be useful in helping with various injuries and conditions.

### Obesity and limited fitness levels

There are many levels of fitness to consider when teaching yoga to children. In some cases limited fitness can be linked to overweight children. It is important to be observant of the children you are working with and make individual modifications based on the child's status as necessary.

# Some general guidelines

***Offer encouragement***. It is important to offer a safe, accepting environment for children, and focus on whatever they can do in the session.

***Encourage children to be compassionate towards themselves and their bodies.*** Many children who have been traumatized, abused, maltreated and/or neglected have low self-esteem. Offer ways in which the children can investigate habitual body patterns and explore new ways of being physical. Safely experimenting with these patterns and discovering healthier and more expansive ways of being embodied will advance self-understanding, engender personal agency and awaken possibility. Building self-esteem is a key aspect of yoga for children.

***Foster greater body awareness.*** Many children who have been traumatized, abused, maltreated and/or neglected disassociate from their bodies as a coping mechanism. Yoga can be beneficial for these children because it helps them to re-inhabit their bodies and relate to their bodies in a healthy and compassionate way. Throughout the yoga practice, ask children to notice how they feel in their bodies. Once they have developed some body awareness, you can encourage them to work at their "edge". This is where they feel they are challenging their bodies but not forcing or straining.

***Incorporate simple standing poses and floor based poses.*** Deep twists, lunges, sun salutations, inversions, and arm balances can be difficult for many children. Instead, focus on simple standing poses such as warrior poses, chair pose, and mountain pose, in addition to floor based poses such as bridge pose and simple lying twists with legs extended farther from the torso than in the traditional version of the poses.

***Start simply and progress gradually.*** Begin with simple poses, gradually progress to more difficult poses as children begin to gain strength and flexibility. Be sure children have built enough strength to move on to more challenging poses. Children have to be mindful of not exerting too much pressure on their joints, as they may be more susceptible to injury if they progress to a pose too quickly.

***Focus on breathing and relaxation.*** Breathing and relaxation can be practiced by all children, and can be the most powerful and effective tools in yoga to manage stress and promote a sense of well-being. Spend time in the session dedicated to breathing practices and deep relaxation, so children can feel a sense of accomplishment and peace in every yoga session. The ultimate goal is to find inner peace, so it is important to include practices that all children can easily and successfully participate in.

***Take a strength-based approach.*** Focus more on what students can do, rather than on what they cannot do. Give praise for everything they accomplish during the group session, and praise even the slightest improvement in a pose. Your goal as facilitators is to support the children in their successes and growth, and you can best accomplish this by making sure they know you believe in them.

***Focus on providing a fun, enjoyable experience for children.***
Most of all, we want children to enjoy the experience of yoga and leave the session feeling relaxed and happy. Don't worry about children being able to do every yoga pose perfectly.

***Be more process-oriented than goal-oriented.*** Encourage children to have fun experimenting with their bodies, instead of being so focused on the outcome of a perfect yoga pose. Incorporate games, partner poses, relaxation and affirmations to build self-esteem and to provide an enjoyable experience for them.

***Offer variations and modifications of poses.*** It is helpful to offer modifications of poses if children are not able to come into the traditional version of the pose. Modifications can be practiced by using blocks, belts, blankets or bolsters. Remind children that yoga is not a competition and that whatever they can do is perfect.

## Some modifications on poses for children who are overweight:

Listed below are traditional yoga poses with modifications. These modifications are for children who can get up and down off the floor and be on their hands and knees. While these poses may seem simple, they bring great relief to overweight children and can provide a much greater sense of ease in their practice.

***Bow Pose*** Rather than taking hold of the ankles or feet, as in the traditional version of bow pose, children can take hold of their pant legs, or if a strap is available, the strap may be wrapped around the ankles and students can hold onto the strap.

***Tree Pose*** Balance can be an issue for children who are overweight, and it may be difficult to bring the foot above the knee in this pose. Children can place the heel of one foot (while keeping the ball of the foot on the floor) on the ankle of the standing leg in this pose to provide more stability. If the child feels balanced, he/she can bring the foot up to the ankle of the standing leg.

***Child's Pose*** If the child can easily get down on their hands and knees, they can open the knees and feet as much as needed to lower back toward the heels and drop the belly and chest toward the floor. If the head doesn't touch the floor, they can make fists with the hands, stacking them on top of each other and letting the head rest on the hands.

***Forward Bends*** Standing or seated forward bends can be difficult for overweight children. If this is the case, they may separate their legs more to allow more space for the abdomen, or if blocks are available for a seated forward bend, two blocks may be stacked for children to rest their heads on. This activates the relaxation response in the body even if children aren't able to come into a full forward bend.

***Relaxation Pose*** Rather than stretching the legs out straight, children can bend their knees and bring their feet closer to their buttocks to take pressure off the lower back. Knees can be touching or close, with feet a little apart, pigeon-toed style, to add back support.

***Using the Wall and/or Chairs*** For overweight children who have a difficult time getting up and down from the floor, it is useful to practice poses from a seated position in a chair, and to use the wall for extra stability for standing poses and forward bends.

# Appendix E: Yoga Postures

**Standing Poses:**

**Mountain/ Tadasana:** Stand tall with your arms by your sides. Feel the top of your head reaching toward the sky and your feet rooting down into the earth. Imagine you are a strong mountain.

**Mountain/Tadasana (arms up variation):** Begin in Mountain pose. Stand tall. Reach your arms over your head and touch your hands. Look at your hands. *Option: Mountain Side Bends:* Stand tall. Reach your arms over your head and touch your hands. Reach your arms up and over and bend your body to the side. Repeat on the other side.

**Standing Forward Bend (Uttanasana):** Stand tall. Reach your arms over your head and touch your hands. Bend over your legs and reach your fingers to the ground. Look at your feet. *Option: Gorilla:* Bend over your legs and hold onto your elbows. Swing from side to side like a gorilla.

**Half Forward Bend (Ardha Uttanasana):** Bend over your legs and reach your fingers to the ground. Look forward and stretch your back long.

**Triangle (Utthita Trikonasana):** Step your feet wide apart. Turn your right toes out and your left toes in. Reach your arms out with your palms facing down. Bend sideways over your right leg and place your right hand on your ankle. Reach your left arm to the sky and look at your raised hand. Repeat on the other side. *Prop Option:* Bring a block to the outside of your right foot and put your hand on the block.

**Warrior I (Virabhadrasana I):** Step your feet wide apart. Turn your right toes out and your left toes in. Bend your right knee and reach your arms over your head, bringing your hands to touch. Repeat the pose on the other side.

**Warrior II (Virabhadrasana II):** Step your feet wide apart. Turn your right toes out and your left toes in. Bend your right knee and stretch your arms out to your sides. Look at your right hand. Imagine you are a strong warrior. Repeat on the other side.

**Devotional Warrior:** Step your feet wide apart. Turn your right toes out and your left toes in. Bend your right knee and interlace your fingers behind your back. Fold forward and bring your head toward your front foot. Let your arms reach over your head.

**Standing Wide-Legged Forward Bend (Prasarita Padottanasana):** Put your hands on your hips and step your feet wide apart. Keep your back straight and bend forward. Place your hands on the floor underneath your shoulders. Bend your knees a little if needed. *Option:* Bring your hands onto blocks placed under your shoulders.

**Twisting Wide-Legged Standing Forward Bend (Prasarita Padotta-nasana):** Put your hands on your hips and step your feet wide apart. Bend forward and place your fingertips on the ground. Keep your back straight. Reach your right arm up toward the sky. Bring your right arm back to the ground and reach your left arm up to the sky. Imagine you are a windmill.

**Extended Side Angle (Utthita Parshvakonasana):** Step your feet wide apart. Turn your right toes out and your left toes in. Bend your right knee and bring your right elbow to your right thigh. Stretch your left arm up alongside your ear. *Option:* Bring your right hand to the floor or on a block, on the inside or outside of your foot.

**Dragon (Anjaneyasana):** Begin on your hands and knees. Step your left foot between your hands to come into a low lunge. Reach your arms up to the sky, palms facing each other. Repeat on the other side.

**Chair (Utkatasana):** Stand tall with your arms by your sides. Breathe in and reach your arms over your head. Breathe out and bend your knees like you are going to sit on a chair.

**Balancing Poses:**

**Tree (Vrkshasana):** Stand tall and let your feet "root" into the earth. Slide the bottom of your left foot onto the ankle, calf, or thigh of your right leg. Point your left knee out to the side and bring your arms over your head. Breathe and balance. Get creative and explore different positions with your arms. To help with balance, look at one spot on the ground in front of you. Repeat on the other side.

**Warrior III (Virabhadrasana III):** With your hands on your hips lean forward and bring your left leg behind you, balancing on your right foot. Reach your arms forward as you continue to balance on one leg.

**Half Moon (Ardha Chandrasana):** Bend forward and bring your hands to the ground. Move your right hand forward and bring your left hand to your hip. Lift your left leg, opening up your hip toward the left side. Reach your left hand straight up to the sky. For an extra challenge look at your raised hand.

**Dancer (Natarajasana):** Stand in Mountain Pose. Bend your right knee and hold your right ankle. Reach your left arm up to the sky. Take a breath in, and breathe out as you bend forward at your hip, kicking your right leg up and back. Reach your left arm forward.

**Crow (Bakasana):** Begin in a wide squat and bring your arms to the inside of your legs and your hands to the floor in front of you. With your hands on the ground put your shins on your upper arms and lean forward. Begin to balance by lifting one foot off the floor, and then the other, bringing your toes to touch while balancing on your hands and arms. *Option 1:* Bring your feet up onto a block placed behind you. *Option 2*: For a challenge, jump your feet back into Low Plank/Chatturanga, or Plank Pose.

**Eagle (Garudasana):** Begin in Mountain Pose with your feet together. Bend your knees and lower down as if you are going to sit on a chair. Cross your right leg over your left leg and hook your toes around your left calf. Bring your right arm under your left arm, twisting at your elbows and wrists so your palms touch. If balancing is difficult let your right foot touch the earth instead of hooked around your leg. Repeat with opposite legs and arms crossed.

**Seated Poses:**

**Pigeon (Eka Pada Rajakapotasana):** From Downward-Facing Dog, bring your right knee to the mat, behind your right hand. Keep your left leg stretched out straight behind you with your toes pointed. Fold forward and stretch your arms out in front of you. You can also stay up on your fingertips or put your forearms on the mat. Stretch back to Downward-Facing Dog. Take a few deep breaths and repeat on the other side.

**Squat (Malasana):** Step your feet apart and squat down. Put your elbows on the inside of your knees, bringing your hands together. Lift and stretch your torso long. **_Option:_** If your heels are lifted, place them on the edge of the rolled mat, or bring your bottom down to rest on a block.

**Reverse Plank (Purvottanasana):** Sit with your legs straight out in front of you. Place your hands behind you with your fingers facing your back. Point your toes and keep them on the ground while you lift your body toward the sky. Relax your head and neck back if it feels comfortable. **_Option:_** You may choose to bend your knees, coming into Tabletop Pose.

**Turtle (Kurmasana):** Sit with the soles of your feet together and your knees apart to make a diamond shape with your legs. Slide your arms under your knees so your palms are facing down on the outside of your legs. Round your back and stretch your head toward your feet. If possible, hold onto the outside of your feet.

**Butterfly (Baddha Konasana):** Bring the bottoms of your feet together and close to your body. Holding the outsides of your feet, lead with your heart and fold forward over your feet. **_Option:_** Open-Winged Butterfly: Begin in Butterfly Pose, holding your big toes. Stretch one leg at a time out to the side until both of your legs are lifted, and you are balancing on your bottom. Keep your spine straight and your stomach muscles strong. Challenge yourself by rolling on your back and coming back into Butterfly Pose without using your hands to lift you up.

**Simple Seated Twist:** Starting in a cross-legged position, breathe in and lift your back, breathe out, and bring your right hand to the outside of your left thigh and your left hand behind your back, close to your bottom. Turn to the left, keeping your back tall. Lift higher with every breath in, and twist more with every breath out. Repeat on the other side.

**Seated Forward Bend (Paschimottanasana):** Sit with your back long and your legs straight out in front of you. Reach your arms up to the sky, making an "L" shape with your body. Fold forward, reaching for your feet while keeping your back straight.

**Wide-Legged Forward Bend (Prasarita Padottanasana):** Sit with your back straight and your legs open wide with your heels on the ground. As you breathe out, fold forward from your waist, leading with your heart and keeping your chest open and back long. Walk your fingers out in front. You can bend your knees slightly in this pose if it feels more comfortable on your lower back. Keep your feet flexed with your toes pointing up, and squeeze your leg muscles so they are strong.

**Head-to-Knee Pose (Janusirsasana):** Sit with your right leg stretched out. Press the bottom of your left foot to the inside of your upper right leg. Fold forward over your straight leg while leading with your heart and keeping your back long. Place your hands on either side of your straight leg, or hold your ankle or foot. Repeat on the other side.

**Lotus (Padmasana):** Sit in a crossed-legged position. Pick up your right foot and place it on top of your upper left leg. Pick up your left foot and place it on top of your upper right leg. ***Options: Easiest:*** Sit in a cross-legged position. If you have trouble keeping your back straight, sit on a rolled mat or a block. ***Easy:*** Place one foot on top of your thigh to sit in Half Lotus. ***Harder:*** While in Full Lotus, place your hands on the floor and lift your bottom off the floor to swing back and forth.

**Seated Cat and Cow:** Sit comfortably and place your hands on your shins or thighs. As you breathe in extend your chest out and shoulders back (Cow pose back). As you breathe out tuck your chin into your chest, rounding your shoulders and back (Cat Pose back). Continue moving back and forth for several breaths.

**Core Poses:**

**Plank (Kumbhakasana):** Come to your hands and knees. Place your hands under your shoulders. Tuck your toes under and push up onto your hands and feet. Keep your arms, legs, and stomach strong.

**Low Plank (Chatturanga Dandasana):** From Plank Pose, or high push up position, bend your elbows and lower to a few inches from the ground. ***Option:*** Keep your knees on the floor.

**Side Plank (Vasisthasana):** Begin in Plank Pose. Shift onto the outside of your right foot, stacking your left foot on top. Bring your left arm to your left hip as you open your body to the left. Extend your left arm to the sky and balance. Repeat on the other side. ***Option:*** If this is difficult, place your top foot down in front of your extended leg for support.

**Boat (Navasana):** Sit on your bottom and hug your knees to your chest, keeping your feet on the ground. Put your hands on the floor behind your back and point your toes. Lift your bent legs and stretch your arms alongside your legs while balancing on your bottom. For a challenge, straighten your legs to make a "V" shape.

**Cat (Marjaryasana):** Begin on your hands and knees, placing your hands under your shoulders with your knees apart and below your hips. Breathe out and round your back as you reach it toward the sky and look at your belly button. Breathe in and come back to starting position. This pose can be practiced with Cow Pose so that you move from one pose to the other.

**Cow (Bitilasana):** Begin on your hands and knees, placing your hands under your shoulders with your knees apart and below your hips. Breathe in as you arch your back and look up. Breathe out and come back to starting. This pose can be practiced with Cat Pose so that you flow from one pose to the other.

**Back-Bending Poses:**

**Cobra (Bhujangasana):** Lie on your belly, placing your hands under your shoulders so your fingertips are in line with the tops of your shoulders. Lead with your heart as you press into your hands and lift your upper body off the earth. Point your toes and squeeze your leg muscles.

**Upward Dog (Urdhva Mukha Svanasana):** Lie on your stomach, stretching your legs back with the tops of your feet on the mat. Place your hands under your shoulders so your fingertips are in line with the tops of your shoulders. Press down into your hands and feet as you lift your body off the earth. Keep your legs strong and your knees lifted off the mat.

**Bridge (Setu Bandha Sarvangasana):** Lie flat on your back with your arms by your sides. Bend your knees, bringing your feet below your knees. Push your feet into the mat as you lift your hips up toward the sky, lifting your back off the mat. Tuck your shoulders and interlace your fingers below your back, keeping your chest open. Keep your legs and your core strong.

**Wheel (Urdhva Dhanurasana):** Lie flat on your back, bend your knees, and place your feet on the earth a few inches from your bottom. Place your hands alongside your ears with your fingers pointing toward your shoulders. Lift your body by pushing into your feet and lifting your hips toward the sky, followed by pushing into your hands and lifting your belly and chest toward the sky. Lastly, lift your head off the ground and relax your neck. When coming down from your wheel pose, tuck your chin into your chest and slowly lower your head, upper back, and lower back to the floor.

**Bow (Dhanurasana):** Lie on your belly and bend your knees so that the bottom of your feet face the ceiling. Reach back with your hands and grab the outside of your ankles. Push your ankles against your hands which will lift your chest and knees off the floor. After a few breaths, come down and rest a few seconds while placing one cheek on the ground.

**Inversion Poses:**

**Downward-Facing Dog (Adho Mukha Svanasana):** Come onto your hands and knees with your hands a little forward of your shoulders and your knees underneath your hips. Press into your hands, curl your toes under, and lift your hips up and back. Keep your legs straight and strong while moving your heels toward the earth. **Horse Kicks**: Come into Downward-Facing Dog and kick your legs into the air one at a time. **Jump-Through:** Start in Downward-Facing Dog Pose. Bend your knees and look forward as you lift your bottom up toward the sky. Press your hands into the floor and jump your legs through your arms, bringing them out straight between your hands to come into a sitting position. *Option:* Use a block under each hand.

**L Dog:** Come into Downward-Facing Dog with your heels against a wall. Place your weight into your hands, keep your arms straight, and take a few steps up the wall. Press your feet into the wall and straighten your legs. Your shoulders should be over your hands and your feet should be at the same height as your hips, creating an "L" shape.

**Dolphin:** Come onto your hands and knees. Lower onto your forearms and interlace your fingers while keeping your elbows shoulder-distance apart. Keep your toes curled under. Push up onto your toes and straighten your legs with your heels reaching toward the mat. Keep your bottom reaching up and look between your feet.

**Handstand (Adho Mukha Vrksasana):** Come into a Downward-Facing Dog with the palms of your hands on the floor about one inch away from a wall. Bend one knee and take a few horse kicks before you try to reach one leg at a time onto the wall, so your heels touch the wall. Keep your feet flexed, squeeze your stomach muscles, and look between your hands. Try balancing by taking one heel off the wall at a time.

**Restorative Poses:**

**Child's Pose (Balasana):** Kneel on the ground and bring your big toes to touch. Separate your knees and gently lay your torso down between your legs, bringing your forehead to the ground. Walk your hands out in front of you, stretching your arms. Take five deep breaths. You can also practice this pose with your arms by your sides with your palms facing up. **Wide-kneed Child's Pose:** Sit on your knees, bring your feet together with big toes touching, and take your knees wider than hip-distance apart. Breathe out and lower your torso down toward the floor, stretching your arms out in front of you.

**Lying Twist:** Lie flat on your back and bring both knees into the chest. Open your arms wide to the sides and slowly take the knees to one side of the body and hold for a few breaths. Turn your head in the opposite direction. Repeat on the other side.

**Thread the Needle (Parsva Balasana):** Start on your hands and knees. Reach your left arm up to the sky and thread it through the space between your right arm and leg. Let your weight sink into your left shoulder as it makes contact with the floor. Come back to your hands and knees and repeat on the other side.

**Hands and knees side stretch:** Start on your hands and knees, keep¬ing your hips above the knees, wrists stacked underneath the shoul¬ders. Take a deep inhale. Exhale and turn your head to the right looking towards your right foot, feeling a stretch on the side of the waist. Inhale back to center, exhale repeat looking to the left at the left foot.

**Puppy Pose (Uttana Shishosana):** Come to your hands and knees while keeping your hips over your knees. Walk your hands forward and rest your forehead on the floor. Keep your arms long with your elbows off the floor and lengthen your back.

**Relaxation Pose (Savasana):** Lay flat on your back with your legs long and your palms facing the sky. Turn your head gently from side to side to stretch your neck. Find a comfortable position for your neck in the center. Gently close your eyes and relax your eyebrows and all the muscles in your face and body. Allow your body to breathe naturally and relax.

**Breathing Poses:**

**Belly Breathing:** Come into a simple cross-legged seated position with your hands together in front of your heart. Breathe in through your nose as you let your belly inflate and fill with air. Exhale through your nose as you let your belly release all the air out, feeling your belly getting smaller.

**Three-Part Breathing:** Lie on your back and place one hand on your belly and the other hand on your chest. Breathe in through your nose as you let your lower belly expand, then your rib cage and then your chest, breathe out through your nose as you release the air out of your chest, rib cage, and belly. Repeat the sequence of bringing air into and out of your lower belly, rib cage, and chest. Focus on your breath and relax. This pose can be practiced lying down or with your legs up the wall. To come into **Legs-Up-the-Wall Pose (Viparita Karani)**, sit with your right side touching the wall. Gently lie back onto the earth as you swing your legs up the wall so they are straight.

**Lion's Breath:** Kneel on the floor with your knees and feet touching and the tops of your feet on the floor. Lower your bottom onto your heels. This is Hero's Pose. Keep your spine straight, your chest open, and drop your shoulders away from your ears. Breathe in through your nose and open your mouth wide as you exhale, sticking out your tongue and making a "ha" sound. Take five Lion's Breaths, letting stiffness release.

**Drain:** This breathing can be practiced either standing or seated. Stretch your arms out in front of you with your fists tightly clenched. Inhale through your nose and tighten all of your muscles in your arms, hands, face, chest, and shoulders. Then, exhale through your mouth while relaxing all of the muscles in your body as you let go of any stress. (Drain breathing is adapted from a program called Conscious Discipline.®)

**Balloon Breathing:** Begin in a seated position. Raise your arms up and interlace your fingers above your head. Place your interlaced hands on your head. As you inhale several breaths of air through your nose, move your hands up toward the sky as if you are blowing up a balloon. When you can't breathe in any more, breathe out through your mouth and let the air out as your arms come down by your sides. (Balloon breathing is adapted from a program called Conscious Discipline.®)

**STAR Breathing:** Come into STAR pose by jumping your feet wide apart. Reach both arms out to the sides. Now be a STAR... (S) Smile (T) Take a big breath in through your nose (A) And pause before (R) Relaxing your arms to your sides as you exhale through your mouth. (STAR breathing is adapted from a program called Conscious Discipline.®)

# Appendix F: Yoga Postures and Breathing for Specific Health Concerns

**Poses for Specific Aliments (Adapted from Teen Yoga Teacher Training Intensive Course Manual) (Wilson, 2010)**

| Ailment | Yoga Posture | Breathing |
|---|---|---|
| Anxiety | Child's Pose<br>Seated Forward Bends<br>Reclined Twists | Three Part-Breathing<br>Belly Breathing |
| Asthma | Fish Pose<br>Upward Dog Pose<br>Cobra Pose | Three Part-Breathing |
| Back Ache | Cat/Cow Pose<br>Lying Twists<br>Plank | Belly Breathing |
| Colds | Turtle Pose<br>Sphinx Pose | Belly Breathing |
| Constipation/Digestion | Wide-Knee Child's Pose<br>Wide-Legged Forward Bend & Twisting<br>Wide-Legged Standing Forward Bend | Belly Breathing |
| Depression | Sun Salutations<br>Lion Pose<br>Warrior Poses | Rapid Diaphragmatic Breathing |
| Fatigue | Handstand<br>Bow Pose | Three Part-Breathing |
| Headache | Bridge Pose<br>Legs up the wall<br>Seated Forward Bend | Belly Breathing |
| Insomnia | Lying Twists<br>Legs-Up-The Wall Pose | Belly Breathing |
| Menstruation | Bow Pose<br>Bridge Pose<br>Seated Forward Bend | Belly Breathing |
| Stomach Ache | Child's Pose<br>Downward Dog Pose | Three Part-Breathing |

# Appendix G: reachwithin Questionnaire

**PART 1: Assessment for before you begin your reachwithin Group session:**

Circle the number that corresponds with your impression of the children in your group

1) On a scale from 0-10, please rate the group of children in your **reachwithin** group on their ability to regulate their emotions, where 0=not able to regulate their emotions, 5= sometimes able to regulate their emotions and 10=always able to regulate their emotions.

0        1        2        3        4        5        6        7        8        9        10

2) On a scale from 0-10, please rate the group of children in your **reachwithin** group on their level of participation, where 0=never participated, 5= sometimes participated and 10=always participated.

0        1        2        3        4        5        6        7        8        9        10

3) On a scale from 0-10, please rate the group of children in your **reachwithin** group on their ability to listen to instructions, where 0=never listened, 5= sometimes listened and 10=always listened.

0        1        2        3        4        5        6        7        8        9        10

4) On a scale from 0-10, please rate the group of children in your **reachwithin** group on their awareness of their emotions, where 0=completely unaware of their emotions, 5= sometimes aware of their emotions and 10=always aware of their emotions.

0        1        2        3        4        5        6        7        8        9        10

5) On a scale from 0-10, please rate the group of children in your **reachwithin** group on their ability to communicate effectively, where 0=never able to communicate effectively, 5= sometimes able to communicate effectively and 10=always able to communicate effectively.

0        1        2        3        4        5        6        7        8        9        10

6) On a scale from 0-10, please rate the group of children in your **reachwithin** group on their ability to work together as a group, where 0=never worked together as a group, 5= sometimes worked together and 10=always worked together as a group.

0        1        2        3        4        5        6        7        8        9        10

7) On a scale from 0-10, please rate the group of children in your **reachwithin** group on their knowledge of yoga, where 0=unknowledgeable about yoga, 5= some awareness of yoga and 10=very knowledgeable about yoga

0        1        2        3        4        5        6        7        8        9        10

8) On a scale from 0-10, please rate the group of children in your **reachwithin** group on their performance of yoga postures, where 0=unable to perform yoga postures or poor performance, 5= sometimes successful at yoga postures or adequate performance and 10=very successful at performance of yoga postures.

0        1        2        3        4        5        6        7        8        9        10

9) On a scale from 0-10, please rate the group of children in your **reachwithin** group on their level of openness and sharing in the group, where 0=no group sharing/very guarded, 5= some group sharing/openness and 10=very open and willing to share with one another.

0        1        2        3        4        5        6        7        8        9        10

10) On a scale from 0-10, please rate the group of children in your **reachwithin** group on their level of participation, where 0=never participated, 5= sometimes participated and 10=always participated.

0        1        2        3        4        5        6        7        8        9        10

*Please answer the following questions for your reachwithin Group:*

1) What stands out most to you in terms of what you would like the children to gain from the group experience?

2) What do you believe strengths are of the children in your group?

3) What special accommodations are you aware of the children you are working with and how will you adjust the group to meet those needs?

**PART 2: Assessment for after your reachwithin Group has ended:**

Circle the number that corresponds with your impression of the children in your group

1) On a scale from 0-10, please rate the group of children in your **reachwithin** group on their ability to regulate their emotions, where 0=not able to regulate their emotions, 5= sometimes able to regulate their emotions and 10=always able to regulate their emotions.

0    1    2    3    4    5    6    7    8    9    10

2) On a scale from 0-10, please rate the group of children in your **reachwithin** group on their level of participation, where 0=never participated, 5= sometimes participated and 10=always participated.

0    1    2    3    4    5    6    7    8    9    10

3) On a scale from 0-10, please rate the group of children in your **reachwithin** group on their ability to listen to instructions, where 0=never listened, 5= sometimes listened and 10=always listened.

0    1    2    3    4    5    6    7    8    9    10

4) On a scale from 0-10, please rate the group of children in your **reachwithin** group on their awareness of their emotions, where 0=completely unaware of their emotions, 5= sometimes aware of their emotions and 10=always aware of their emotions.

0    1    2    3    4    5    6    7    8    9    10

5) On a scale from 0-10, please rate the group of children in your **reachwithin** group on their ability to communicate effectively, where 0=never able to communicate effectively, 5= sometimes able to communicate effectively and 10=always able to communicate effectively.

0    1    2    3    4    5    6    7    8    9    10

6) On a scale from 0-10, please rate the group of children in your **reachwithin** group on their ability to work together as a group, where 0=never worked together as a group, 5= sometimes worked together and 10=always worked together as a group.

0    1    2    3    4    5    6    7    8    9    10

7) On a scale from 0-10, please rate the group of children in your **reachwithin** group on their knowledge of yoga, where 0=unknowledgeable about yoga, 5= some awareness of yoga and 10=very knowledgeable about yoga.

0      1      2      3      4      5      6      7      8      9      10

8) On a scale from 0-10, please rate the group of children in your **reachwithin** group on their performance of yoga postures, where 0=unable to perform yoga postures or poor performance, 5= sometimes successful at yoga postures or adequate performance and 10=very successful at performance of yoga postures.

0      1      2      3      4      5      6      7      8      9      10

9) On a scale from 0-10, please rate the group of children in your **reachwithin** group on their level of openness and sharing in the group, where 0=no group sharing/very guarded, 5= some group sharing/openness and 10=very open and willing to share with one another.

0      1      2      3      4      5      6      7      8      9      10

10) On a scale from 0-10, please rate the group of children in your **reachwithin** group on their level of participation, where 0=never participated, 5= sometimes participated and 10=always participated.

0      1      2      3      4      5      6      7      8      9      10

### *Please answer the following questions about your experience of your reachwithin Group*

1) Please give some feedback regarding any needs or concerns you had during the group experience, and/or any changes you would like to make for the group experience?

2) What if anything did you observe regarding the strengths of the children you worked within your **reachwithin** Group?

3) What if anything did you observe regarding weaknesses or biggest challenges for the children you worked with or for the group experience as a whole?

4) Please note any successes or difficulties regarding accommodating special situations/needs that arose for the children in your group.

5) What did you find the most helpful in preparing and leading the **reachwithin** group? What suggestions do you have for what would be helpful in the future for other facilitators or for the next **reachwithin** group you facilitate?

6) What recommendations do you have moving forward for the children in your **reachwithin** group?

# XII. References

Bailey, B. (2011). *Creating the School Family*. Oviedo, Florida: Loving Guidance, Inc.

Blaustein, M. E., & Kinniburgh, K. M. (2010). *Treating traumatic stress in children and adolescents*. New York: The Guilford Press.

Brazelton, T. B. (2006). *Touchpoints*. (2nd ed.). Boston, MA: Da Capo Press.

Caron, J.W. Connections child and Adolescent Group Program. Retrieved June 12, 2012, from http://connectionscagp.com.

Clausen, J. M., Landsverk, J., et al. (1998). *Mental health problems of children in foster care*. Journal of Child and Family Studies, 7, 283-296.

Cooper, J.L., Banghart, P., Aratani, P. (2010). *Addressing the Mental Health Needs of Young Children in the Child Welfare System: What every Policymaker Should Know*. New York, New York. The National Center for Children in Poverty.

Hennessey, M. (2011). *Mental Health/Psychosocial Needs Assessment for Institutionalized Youth in Grenada; a REACH Grenada Report*. New York, New York: REACH Grenada.

Khouri, H. (2008). *Mind-Body Resources for Working with Those at Risk*. 2nd Edition. Los Angeles, California: Yoga Ed.

Lilly, M., Arrants, K., Turley, L., Southcote, C. (2012). *Street Yoga Teacher Trainig Manual*. Portland, Oregon: Street Yoga.

Lowenstein, L. (1999). *Creative Interventions for Troubled Children & Youth*. Toronto, Canada: Liana Lowenstein.

Saxe, G. N., Ellis, B. H., & Kaplow, J. B. (2007). *Collaborative treatment of traumatized children and teens*. New York, NY: The Guilford Press.

Sears, M., Sears, W. (1995). *The discipline book: how to have a better-behaved child from birth to age ten*. New York, New York: Little, Brown and Company.

Vilchez-Baltt, S., Hester-Smith, A., Phillips, J. (2008). *Karma Kids Yoga Teacher Training Course Manual*. New York, New York: Karma Kids Yoga.

Wilson, E., Vilchez-Baltt, S., Phillips, J., Oppenheimer, J.F. (2010). *Teen Yoga Teacher Training Intensive Course Manual*. New York, New York: Karma Kids Yoga.

World Health Organization (2011, October). Mental health: a state of well-being. www.who.int/features/factfiles/mental_health/en/. Retrieved November 4, 2011, from http://www.who.int/features/factfiles/mental_health/en/.

"Child Development Tracker." PBS for Parents. PBS, 2012. Web. 3 Oct 2012. Ibid.

"Stages of Adolescent Development." HeadStart: An Office of the Administration for Children and Families Early Childhood Learning & Knowledge Center 2008. Web. 3 Oct 2012. <eclkc.ohs.acf.hhs. gov/hslc/tta...

# XIII. Glossary

**Asana:** The Sanskrit word for yoga posture. Sanskrit is the ancient language of yoga.

**Coping skills:** Skills, techniques, behaviors and actions we use to help us adjust to change and manage stressors or demands of everyday life.

**Emotional literacy:** The ability to identify and understand feelings and emotions.

**Hatha:** The type of yoga that focuses on the physical postures and breathing exercises.

**Karma yoga:** Is considered to be a type of yoga where the practice is of helping others.

**Meditation**: A practice where you spend time in quiet in order to quiet your mind and thoughts.

**Pranayama:** The Sanskrit word for breathing practices used in yoga.

**Resilience:** A child's ability to "bounce back" from stress and difficult life experiences.

**Self-regulation:** The ability to notice and tolerate difficult feelings, and manage mood or behavior.

**Social skills:** The ability to communicate with others, form relationships, and participate in community.

**Yoga:** Physical postures and breathing exercises that are good for both the body and the mind. The word yoga is the Sanskrit word for union. In the practice of yoga you unite your mind, body and spirit.

# XIV. Lesson Plans

This section of the manual includes sample lesson plans for each of the 12 topic areas covered in the **reachwithin** program. The following sample lessons are a resource and framework for moving forward.

Please refer to Chapter III (The **reachwithin** Model) for detailed information on the program structure. Each lesson contains an opening, yoga postures, main activity, relaxation and closing.

For the yoga portion of this program, four yoga sequences have been developed to suit the needs of this population. Sequence 1 is used for topics 1-3, sequence 2 for topics 4-6, sequence 3 for topics 7-9 and sequence 4 for topics 10-12. This design allows both the facilitator and children to build competency in the sequences while also keeping the material new and interesting. Each yoga sequence contains postures to warm the body up, a challenge pose and a yoga game.

The activity section includes material for two to four different activities. This provides the facilitator with a choice of activity when teaching the lesson.

Lessons may be adjusted as appropriate for your setting and participants. See section below for how to adjust for different ages.

## Using reachwithin with different ages

**reachwithin** was created to be used primarily with children from 8 to 12 years of age, but can be used with younger and older children by thinking creatively and taking into account some tips and suggestions to make it appropriate for children of different ages.

When adjusting the program to work with the age group of children you work with ask yourself the following: Are there any topic areas that are more or less important for the group I work with? How long can the children I work with sit or focus for? What are their general interests and activities they like to do? Are there certain ways the children I work with learn best (by writing, drawing, talking, working individually or working as a group)? What would I have been interested in doing or learning when I was their age?

The answers to these questions will give you extra information to help adjust the group lesson plans to work with your group. When you look at the lesson plans ask yourself: Do I need to adjust the messages so it is better understood by my group of children? Which activities can I keep and which ones should I change? You may find that you can keep the activities and main communication points but have to change the meditation or closing activity. Be creative and try things out.

Be sure to review what you can expect from children at different ages and stages (found in Chapter VII and appendix B) so you can make some adjustments for your group.

Here are a few helpful hints to keep in mind when working with younger children:

- Young children may have trouble sitting for extended periods of time, so think about making the group session shorter.
- Children learn well through examples, so identify a children's book that you can read for each topic.
- Keep the children active and moving.
- Young children may struggle with writing activities. With this in mind, try to substitute writing with drawing (for example, ask the children to draw a picture of their strengths or of their goals)
- Invite the children to use their imagination and incorporate some role playing or pretending whenever possible.
- Children learn best when rules and expectations are clear and consistent.
- Make sure you provide frequent positive reinforcement in order to keep the children engaged and motivated.


Here are a few helpful tips to consider when working with older children:

- Older children are working on relationships and identity, so encouraging more talking and discussion can be powerful.
- Consider extending the length of the group session so there is enough time to really focus in on the material.
- Allow for individual journal time at each session or invite children to write their own stories about their experiences with a specific theme.
- Encourage older children to role-play so they can gain experience working with the themes they are learning about.
- Assign children appropriate responsibilities so they can help run their own group sessions, therefore encouraging and fostering positive leadership skills.
- Make sure you provide frequent positive reinforcement in order to keep the children focused, interested and motivated.


## Session Preparation

Here are some tips to be best prepared for group sessions.

The day before each group session:
- Read through the sample lesson plan two times, make notes on any adjustments that are needed, and practice the activity yourself before the group.
- Collect all the materials needed for class (for example, iPod, speakers, books, props, etc.)
- Ask yourself, "am I familiar with the main teaching points? Do I know all of the yoga poses, breathing exercises, and activities?  Am I familiar enough that I will not need to constantly refer back to the outline during the session?"

On the day of the group session:
- Try to arrive 30 minutes before the beginning of the session to set up the room, organize the children and yourself. You may want to review the class plan for the day and make sure that all props are in order (e.g. mats set up, etc), do yoga or focus yourself to let go of any worries or concerns that you may bring into the session.

When preparing children for the group:
- Make sure that children dress in loose, comfortable clothing that allow them to move and stretch when possible. If the children do not dress appropriately (or in a provocative way) remember not to shame them for what they wear. Simply remind them of the dress rule, which means comfortable, loose, clothing.
- Encourage the children to use the bathroom before the group starts to avoid group interruptions.

Printed in the United States
By Bookmasters